Praise for Expecting the Unexpected

In *Expecting the Unexpected*, Blair Meeks has given us profound yet gentle insights into the many dimensions of Advent. Through the beauty of the written prayers, the clarity and simplicity of the study structure, and the astute reflections on the Advent texts, she provides substantive material for an individual or a group to experience Advent in new and unexpected ways. She lifts up the sense in which Advent, like an intense white light holding all other colors within it, embraces every aspect of Christ's ministry and person. And she never loses sight of the practical implications of Advent for our own Christlike actions in our world. What a gift this book is, for Advent, Christmas, or any season!

—MARJORIE HEWITT SUCHOCKI
Professor Emerita, Claremont School of Theology

If you feel trapped by a romanticized Christmas gospel, Blair Meeks's invitation to *expect the unexpected* is your escape hatch. But beware! You will likely never observe Advent or celebrate Christmas "like the ones you used to know." She doesn't do all of the work for you. She simply gives you markers and turns you over to the Holy Spirit and surprise!

—DANIEL BENEDICT
Writer and Consultant, Worship and Liturgy
Former director of Worship Resources
General Board of Discipleship
The United Methodist Church

Expecting the Unexpected

Unexpected

AN ADVENT DEVOTIONAL GUIDE

BLAIR GILMER MEEKS

UPPER
ROOM BOOKS®
NASHVILLE

For Kathryn, Betty Jean, and Philip
singers of the hymns,
keepers of the stories,
and lovers of God's justice

Contents

Introduction

❦

PRAISING GOD IN A STRANGE LAND

> *O sing to the* LORD *a new song,*
> *for [God] has done marvelous things.*
>
> — PSALM 98:1

This psalm, traditionally read on Christmas Day, invites us to celebrate again the coming of God into our lives, to sing with joy in thanksgiving for the new thing God is doing through Jesus Christ. But how can we make a joyful noise when the world's troubles seem to gather like storm clouds around us, bringing anxiety and fear? How can we sing for joy when we carry sadness in our hearts, when we live daily with news of war, disaster, and brokenness both far away and close to home? The words of a different psalm may ring truer to our times: "How could we sing the LORD's song in a foreign land?" (Ps. 137:4).

We do live in a strange, foreign land, even if the houses, the landscape, and the people around us are familiar. Those of us who look for God's coming often feel like strangers in our own land. During this holy season of Advent, we watch public festivities whose main purpose seems to be to encourage us to join the frantic Christmas shopping marathon. All year long a cacophony of confusing stories spins all around us, usually hyping the exploits of our culture's preoccupation with entertainers and sports heroes. We endure the blare of television shows, movies, and commercials that proclaim values alien to our calling in Jesus Christ.

Yet we know the true story—the one of how God has already come in Jesus Christ. This story gives us hope, beginning with the astonishing birth of God's Son to Mary of Nazareth and ending with the promise of Jesus' coming again in clouds of glory to bring his reign of peace. In this promise we find our future—God's future—filled with joy and praise. The Advent season invites us to discover this story again so we can sing along with the old hymn, "Since Christ is Lord of heaven and earth, How can I keep from singing?"[1]

The Advent scriptures are addressed to people who lived in fear. The threat of terrorism was a reality for the exiles in the days of the Hebrew prophets, for those who lived under Rome's heavy hand in Jesus' homeland, and for the scattered early Christians to whom Paul was writing. In our own time, terrorist acts instill fear and shake many nations. The hope of Advent for the healing of the nations, for blessing and well-being for earth's inhabitants, is our greatest longing as we watch news of the unfolding devastation in one place after another. "Through all the tumult and the strife I hear the music ringing; It finds an echo in my soul—How can I keep from singing?"

Advent's promise is sung in the poems of Isaiah and the songs of Luke's Gospel. How can we keep from singing when Advent promises the coming of God's great reversal—swords changed into plowshares, the lowly lifted up and the powerful brought low? Daily we observe around us a culture oblivious to God's life-giving promise, and we experience the reality of "principalities and powers" that defy God's rule of life. But out of all this gloom and fear, we hear Isaiah's invitation: "Come, let us walk in the light of the Lord!" (Isa. 2:5).

CHARLES WESLEY'S HYMNS AND THE SCRIPTURES OF ADVENT

The great hymns of the church we sing during Advent and Christmas open up the scriptures for us. Our eyes may glaze over when someone tries to explain "incarnational theology," but we sing with great feeling Charles Wesley's familiar Christmas hymn, and when we do, we have made a significant statement about the Incarnation:

> Veiled in flesh the Godhead see; hail th' incarnate Deity,
> pleased with us in flesh to dwell, Jesus, our Emmanuel.
> ("Hark! the Herald Angels Sing," stanza 2)

This statement may need some reflection before the meaning is clear to us. We have sung it all our lives and heard it on hundreds of Christmas albums, but do we know what lies behind it? Do we know the scriptures the hymn is based on? Do we know what the church has said for generations about this Jesus who was born a poor baby in a war-torn country, and yet "in him all the fullness of God was pleased to dwell" (Col. 1:19)?

During the weeks of Advent and Christmas, we will look at five hymns of Charles Wesley and study the scripture passages they reflect. No hymn writer has a better sense of the seasons of the church year than did Charles Wesley, and it was his gift to put into his poetry, with its striking imagery and economy of words, a concise and marvelous expression of our faith.

Those of us in the Methodist traditions think of Wesley as our own, but the Anglicans have a prior claim, and every year on a special day in the church calendar they commemorate the contributions of both John and Charles Wesley—who remained Anglican priests. Charles Wesley's hymns are loved and sung by Christians in all denominations and have been translated into many languages. These poetic songs comprise one of the threads that hold us together, reminding us of the unity Christ expected from all his followers. The three hundredth anniversary celebration of this great hymn writer's birth in 1707 reminds us that one of the ways we tell the story of Jesus' birth, life, death, and resurrection is through the words of Charles Wesley's poetry.

How to Use this Book

In order to prepare for celebrating Jesus' coming at Christmas, people of faith should be grounded in a clear understanding of the whole story of Jesus—his life and ministry, his death and resurrection, and the promise of his coming again. *Expecting the Unexpected* offers readings, prayers, background material, images for meditation, and reflection questions to guide the journey of exploring your faith in Christ on a new level. Most significantly, this book encourages you to take this journey with others, recognizing that we come to know Jesus best in the company of his followers.

Each chapter of this book begins with an introduction to the theme for that week, which is the starting point for your reflection at home. Together with the suggestions for daily scripture readings and prayer, the theme essays also suggest a devotional resource and a background study for the weekly small-group sessions. Each participant is asked to set aside a quiet time to read the scriptures, pray, and reflect on the meaning of the scripture readings for this season.

The readings and suggestions in the first four chapters of this book are also useful for individual readers who can't attend small-group sessions and are seeking a devotional guide to read at home. In this case, the leader's guide in chapter 5 can serve as a summary and a guide to further study.

We are called on to use not only our intellect in approaching the scriptures but also our imaginations.

We are called on to use not only our intellect in approaching the scriptures but also our imaginations. When we study scripture with our intellect, we use our analytical skills, along with commentaries and other tools, for understanding the historical context and the various levels of meaning of the words. In addition, we use our imaginations so we can become part of the story and find out what the scripture says for our own time and what promise it holds for our future.

Reading the scripture with imagination, however, does not mean engaging in flights of fancy or adding ideas to the text that are not there. Using our imagination allows us to focus on the images—light, shadow, water, wilderness, potter, clay, holy mountain, lions and lambs, among many rich examples—and enter into the poetry of the Bible. Some of us put away our poetic imaginations after childhood and may find them a bit rusty. But they are still there, lying dormant, and will awaken to the possibilities of these beautiful words as they come alive through prayer and quiet reflection. It helps to pray slowly, beginning with the words of written prayers and adding your own concerns and petitions. Time without distractions is essential for reading and reflecting. Visual art, poetry, and music help stir our imaginative insights. Let us pray that we will open ourselves to being led through the wilderness to streams of living water.

A note about the reflection questions provided for each day: I have written the questions with the idea that not all readers will be interested in the same issues. Choose the questions that intrigue you the most and think about them during the week. At the small-group session, participants will hold a variety of viewpoints and will have considered diverse avenues of exploration individually. Through lively discussion we can all learn from one another. Don't be discouraged if you can't answer all the questions immediately. Significant questions do not necessarily have ready answers. I hope you will enjoy the challenges the questions present, allow them to percolate in your thoughts for a while, and remain open to the ideas they may spark.

The leader's guide includes a plan for five small-group study sessions based on the daily readings each week. Every participant needs a copy of the book and a journal for writing impressions, insights, and questions that occur during the daily readings and prayer. Before coming to the group session, participants may review their journal entries for the week and decide which ideas and questions to bring to the group.

The book uses the following hymnal abbreviations. All the hymn texts in this book come from the *UMH*.

UMH - United Methodist Hymnal
NCH - New Century Hymnal (United Church of Christ)
EH - The Hymnal 1982 (Episcopal Church)
PH - The Presbyterian Hymnal
LBW - Lutheran Book of Worship
TBH - The Baptist Hymnal (1991)
AMECH - African Methodist Episcopal Church Hymnal

First Week of Advent

❧

EXPECTING CHRIST'S NEW CREATION

The one who was seated on the throne said,
"See, I am making all things new."

— REVELATION 21:5

Teachers and parents, trying to encourage a child who is troubled by feelings of inadequacy, sometimes say to the child, "Don't give up. God isn't through with you yet." What is true for children also holds true for adults. Like a potter who isn't satisfied with the way the object on the wheel shapes up, God can take the clay of our lives and remold us into a new creation.

Indeed, God continues working to perfect the whole of God's good creation. We celebrate God's wondrous act of calling the world into being, we sing of God's Spirit sweeping over the waters, and we remember God's word going out: "'Let there be light'; and there was light" (Gen. 1:3). We know that God was pleased with the work of creation and rested, but nowhere does the Bible say that God stopped creating. Quite the opposite: God isn't through with us yet and continually brings newness into our lives. The creator God "has created and is creating," in the words of a statement of faith from the United Church of Canada.

I often wonder how we can decorate our tree, haul out the nativity set, sing "Away in a Manger" once or twice, pack it all away again, and think we have celebrated Christmas adequately. The season holds so much more for us. The babe in the manger is a sign of what God is doing among us here on earth, but God's work through Jesus Christ only *begins* in the manger. Our joy in God's gift of Jesus to us should be part of our lives every day.

What we celebrate during Advent and Christmas is the completely new way God comes to us in Jesus Christ.

First we should ask: Who did this baby grow up to be? His family didn't understand him at first; even John the Baptist began to doubt that this man who ate with sinners and seemed an unlikely hero could be the longed-for Messiah. Unless we know the whole story of Jesus' life, death, and resurrection; unless we ask ourselves what changes in our own lives Jesus' coming brings; unless we anchor our present in the community of Jesus Christ and our future in God's household of life, we haven't celebrated Christmas.

What we celebrate during Advent and Christmas is the completely new way God comes to us in Jesus Christ. We also celebrate the new persons we are becoming because God sent Jesus, God's own beloved Son, to the world God loved so much. We should say one more thing from the start: We also pray that God will finish the new creation, that God will redeem the whole earth and free it "from its bondage to decay" (Rom. 8:21). Our Advent celebrations are based on our hope that God will bring a new heaven and a new earth in which all creatures have everything they need for life and live together in harmony with one another.

To have the courage to pray for God's new creation means to rely on the promises, remember God's "awesome deeds" among us in the past, and look for Jesus Christ's coming again to bring the fullness of his reign of peace. Prayer always combines words and actions, so to pray for Jesus to come in clouds of glory also means to work for Christ's love to shape our world right now.

Advent offers an invitation to reflect on our own relationship with Jesus and prepare to receive him into our lives again. Advent also invites us to remember the urgent reasons for Jesus' coming and God's desire to make a new beginning for the earth and all its peoples. Observing Advent through prayer, Bible study, and reflection doesn't take us away from the world and its troubles, but it does bring us hope and therefore a renewed purpose to work for God's will to be done so that all creatures, even the earth itself, will have life in abundance. Our hope is based on the assurance that Christ has come, Christ is with us, and Christ will come again. We look again for Jesus, the newborn babe in Bethlehem, and for Jesus Christ, the firstborn of the new creation, the Resurrected One who will return in the clouds. What we know about our own future is that "when he is revealed, we will be like him" (1 John 3:2).

Following are scripture readings and ideas for reflection for six days of the week. Find a quiet time and place to read, pray, and meditate every day. As you do, write down your thoughts and questions and think about what insights you would like to share later in the group discussion.

DAILY SCRIPTURE READINGS

Isaiah 2:1-5; Isaiah 11:1-10; Isaiah 64:1-9; Romans 6:1-11; Romans 13:11-14; 2 Corinthians 5:16-21; Philippians 1:3-11; Luke 21:25-28; Revelation 1:4-8; Revelation 21:1-7

PSALM FOR THE WEEK

Read Psalm 25:1-10 aloud every day.

HYMN FOR THE WEEK

"Lo, He Comes with Clouds Descending" (*UMH #718, EH #57–58, PH #6, LBW #27, TBH #199, AMECH #99*)

> Lo, he comes with clouds descending,
> once for favored sinners slain;
> thousand, thousand saints attending
> swell the triumph of his train.
> Hallelujah! Hallelujah! Hallelujah!
> God appears on earth to reign.
>
> Every eye shall now behold him,
> robed in dreadful majesty;
> those who set at naught and sold him,
> pierced and nailed him to the tree,
> deeply wailing, deeply wailing, deeply wailing,
> shall the true Messiah see.
>
> The dear tokens of his passion
> still his dazzling body bears;
> cause of endless exultation
> to his ransomed worshipers;
> with what rapture, with what rapture, with what rapture,
> gaze we on those glorious scars!

Yea, Amen! Let all adore thee,
high on thy eternal throne;
Savior, take the power and glory,
claim the kingdom for thine own.
Hallelujah! Hallelujah! Hallelujah!
Everlasting God, come down!

—CHARLES WESLEY, 1758

This hymn may be unfamiliar to some readers, and worship planners sometimes avoid it because of its difficult references to Christ's second coming. It is, however, a powerful, biblical hymn with several strong musical settings, and it focuses on an aspect of this season that we sometimes neglect: Advent is a time of preparing to celebrate the coming of Jesus as a baby in Bethlehem, but it is also a time to prepare for Christ's second Advent when all God's enemies—even death—will be defeated. You may find this hymn in the Advent section of your hymnal, or you may find it toward the end with other hymns related to the return and reign of Christ.

The hymn's scriptural basis is Revelation 1:7 (and indirectly Dan. 7:13-14), but it also alludes to the Gospel readings in all three years of the lectionary for the first Sunday in Advent. Charles Wesley sees the risen and ascended Christ, still recognizable by the scars of the Crucifixion, being worshiped by all the saints and recognized even by those who opposed him. The theme of full disclosure is another emphasis of Advent: Christ will be fully revealed, and all will know him (Isa. 40:5). When we sing this hymn, we remember Christ's coming, reflect on his crucifixion and resurrection, and expect his coming again in glory.

Day 1

SCRIPTURE

Read Psalm 25:1-10 aloud.
Read Isaiah 2:1-5 and Isaiah 11:1-10.

IMAGES

Let your mind wander to a hillside with green grass and animals grazing. Remember the pleasure of being close to a favorite pet or the beauty of birds at a feeder on a snowy day. Give thanks for animal helpers and friends. Pray for the healing of the earth.

REFLECTIONS

List the images of peace that caught your attention in the two readings from Isaiah. What draws people to God's holy mountain? What characteristics of a just ruler are named in Isaiah 11? What part does knowledge play in both these readings? How can you contribute to a good living environment in your own community? What can we as a church do to be peacemakers?

PRAYER

God of life, your prophet Isaiah knew that you can change weapons of war into tools for peace. Help us become your instruments of reconciliation. Isaiah saw in your home a place where enemies could live in peace—a place for wolves, lambs, leopards, kids, calves, lions, cows, and bears to lie down together. Teach us to care for the earth you created and to work for a safe place for all people and animals to live. In the name of Jesus. Amen.

Day 2

SCRIPTURE

Read Psalm 25:1-10 aloud.
Read Isaiah 64:1-9.

IMAGES

Imagine that you are present with the disciples on the Day of Pentecost. Watch the flames of fire and hear the rushing of the wind as God tears open the heavens and comes down. Imagine the initial noise and confusion, and then feel the peace and understanding that the Holy Spirit brings as it settles on the room.

REFLECTIONS

What does Isaiah's image of God as potter say to us about God's continuing work of forming and changing us? What is creative about God's forgiveness? What does it mean to be God's people? How does God create a community?

PRAYER

Loving God, you sent your Son, Jesus, to break down walls that divide and to bring all people to you. Make us ambassadors of your peace and stewards of all the earth. Help us to live each day filled with grace and in harmony with one another. In the name of the Prince of Peace. Amen.

Day 3

SCRIPTURE

Read Psalm 25:1-10 aloud.
Read Romans 6:1-11 and Romans 13:11-14.

IMAGES

Hold in your mind the sound and feel of running water. Remember your baptism and be thankful. Hold in your mind the image of a shaft of light. In your imagination walk into a sunlit room and feel the warmth of God's face shining on you.

REFLECTIONS

What kind of wake-up call would it take for us to live as if "our salvation is near"? Adult converts in the early church were told to "put on the Lord Jesus Christ" when they emerged from the waters of baptism and received their new robes. How can we put on the Lord Jesus Christ in our lives?

PRAYER

God of glory, you sent Jesus Christ, your Son, to live and die with us; you raised him from the dead and gave him a name that is above every name. Grant us grace to walk with him in newness of life every day and to live in the hope of his coming again to make all things new. In Jesus' name. Amen.

Day 4

Read Psalm 25:1-10 aloud.
Read 2 Corinthians 5:16-21 and Philippians 1:3-11.

IMAGES

Open your mind to a series of images of the compassionate Christ: Jesus blessing children, weeping with Mary and Martha, healing the sick, dying for our sake, eating breakfast with disciples after the Resurrection, blessing the church as he ascends to heaven. Open your mind to a series of images of love overflowing in your community of faith.

REFLECTIONS

What does Paul tell us in 2 Corinthians 5:16-21 about how we look at one another in a new way because of Christ's coming? Think about people you know whose faithful lives affect the way you regard them. In what ways can we bring the message of reconciliation to the world?

What do you think God has in mind for us when we are brought "to completion" (Phil. 1:3-11)? How do we determine "what is best"? What is a "harvest of righteousness"? the "righteousness of God"?

PRAYER

God of wisdom, we know that you have begun a good work in us and that you will bring it to completion. Grant us love that overflows, give us insight, and teach us how to discern what is best. Guide us to work for the glory and praise of God. Through Christ our Lord. Amen.

Day 5

SCRIPTURE

Read Psalm 25:1-10 aloud.
Read Luke 21:25-28 and Revelation 1:4-8.
Read the hymn "Lo, He Comes with Clouds Descending" (p. 18).

IMAGES

Picture in your mind all the possible meanings of the word *end* (examples: a destination or goal, the close of a story). Who is our "end"?

Reflect on Jesus' willingness to leave God's side and come to earth to suffer and die for the world. Reflect on Jesus' return in glory and how we will recognize him.

REFLECTIONS

What do people fear about the "end times"? Why should we not be afraid, according to Luke? What is wrong with popular culture's depiction of Jesus as coming with anger and vengeance to condemn the world? (See John 3:16-17.) In the Gospels, "to see" Jesus means to truly know him, to believe. What do you think "every eye will see him" means in Revelation 1:7?

God of mercy, you alone know the day and the hour of Christ's coming. Keep us awake; give us courage to do your work while we wait. Open our lives to Jesus' advent among us in unexpected ways through all our days. Open our eyes that we may see Jesus and know him. In the name of Jesus, our Savior. Amen.

Day 6

SCRIPTURE

Read Psalm 25:1-10 aloud.
Read Revelation 21:1-7.

IMAGES

Imagine yourself on the shore of an island, watching a chaotic ocean—boiling with angry waves and separating you from all those you love. Imagine the ocean receding and being replaced by a fresh mountain spring flowing with water that tastes good and revives you. Open your heart and mind to feel God's presence with you.

REFLECTIONS

What do you think of the possibility suggested in Revelation that rather than our going "up" to heaven, a new heaven and a new earth will come to us? Where else in the Bible can you find that God's home is with us? (See, for example, 2 Sam. 7:1-11 and John 1:14.)

Think about the sentence, "In the end is the beginning." How does this relate to the reading from Revelation?

PRAYER

We thank you, O God, that you make your home with us and make us your people. We thank you for your life-giving power to raise Jesus from the dead, for your compassion that wipes away all tears. Give us grace to welcome your holy Son, born to reign in us today. Amen.

Second Week of Advent

☙

EXPECTING THE HOPE OF THE EARTH

"Are you the one who is to come,
or are we to wait for another?"

— MATTHEW 11:3

One of the first facts we learn about Jesus is that he was sent from the God of Israel to deliver his own people. Jesus' Jewish heritage is well documented in the Bible. The "Son of David," his genealogy is traced to Abraham in Matthew and to Adam in Luke. On the eighth day after his birth, he was circumcised and then later taken to the Temple, "according to the law of Moses," and dedicated to God (Luke 2:21-40). Revered as a rabbi who knew the scriptures well, Jesus advocated a new interpretation of the law and engaged in the time-honored tradition of debates among scholars. Many of his positions were supported by other Jewish scholars in his own time and later. He was crucified, according to Pilate's instructions (John 19:19), as "King of the Jews," the same title the magi gave him when they came from the East to worship the infant king.

Jesus came to set his people free because he came from God; this is the nature of the God of Israel. We learned this about God already in Exodus 3:7-8 when God came to set the Hebrews free from their slavery in Egypt: "I have observed the misery of my people. . . . I have heard their cry. . . . Indeed, I know their sufferings, and I have come down to deliver them from the Egyptians." For thousands of years oppressed peoples have found their hope in this story and looked to God for deliverance.

In our own time we can see examples of God's will at work to make people free. The abolition and civil rights movements in the United States began in the churches. Black South Africans, segregated and oppressed by the apartheid government, were freed when leaders like Nelson Mandela and Archbishop Desmond Tutu appealed to the conscience of the rest of the world. We also know the role of the church in bringing down the Soviet Empire. The Roman Catholic influence in destroying the communist hold on Poland is often cited, but less well-known acts of courage by Protestant and Orthodox churches in other countries also contributed. The Berlin Wall came down in some measure because the churches in East Germany continued to do what the church always does—they cared for the weak in their society, gathered people to hear Christ's gospel of freedom and hope preached from the pulpit, and held candlelight prayer vigils in the shadow of the monstrous wall. The light of our Advent candles shining in the shadows of our lives reminds us that we celebrate the coming of the Light of the world that no darkness can overcome.

Many people in Jesus' time were expecting a messiah sent from God to free them from Rome's oppression. They were disappointed that Jesus' coming did not immediately signal an end to Roman rule. Rome crumbled and fell several centuries after the apostles began preaching the gospel of Jesus Christ. Many martyrs were willing to die for this gospel. The early followers of Jesus would gain their strength by worshiping in secret and ministering to the poor and the outcast—the "nobodies," in Rome's way of thinking.

Even John the Baptist, the "voice of one crying out in the wilderness: 'Prepare the way of the Lord'" (Luke 3:4), began to have difficulty thinking of Jesus as the promised Messiah. John had been thrown in prison. His simple lifestyle, his fiery preaching, and his admonitions concerning the poor did not endear him to Herod and his queen, the "wife" whom Herod had stolen from his own brother. They did not like being called on to repent, and they were bent on accumulating as much wealth as they could wring out of their poor subjects.

New life in Christ is recognizable by a spiritual awakening and a renewal of individuals and the community.

Isolated in a fortification near the Dead Sea, John must have wondered where Jesus was and why he did not bring down God's wrath on the Roman oppressors and their puppet, King Herod. Instead of condemning and using his "winnowing fork," as John expected, Jesus freed people from physical limitations and also from the limitations imposed by an oppressive society; he healed the sick and disabled, preached good news to the poor, welcomed outcasts into the community, and brought new life to all who came to him. New life in Christ is recognizable by a spiritual awakening and a renewal of individuals and the community.

When John's disciples asked him if he was indeed the One John had expected to be sent from God, Jesus replied by telling them to go and tell John what they saw and heard.

Then Jesus listed the acts attributed to the Messiah in Isaiah 29:18-19 and 35:5-6: "The blind receive their sight, the lame walk, the lepers are cleansed, the deaf hear, the dead are raised, and the poor have good news brought to them" (Matt. 11:5). Jesus did not put aside John's imprisonment and the abuses of the Roman rulers; rather, he pointed to the totality of God's gift of freedom. Bringing good news to those who face disability and poverty, taking care of the least in the kingdom first (v. 11), is where Jesus began, so that all people would be free to enjoy the fullness of life in a community of love. Until the least of our sisters and brothers have freedom, none of us will have freedom.

Rome built highways and used them to create an empire; those highways were an ever-present reminder of Rome's power. In contrast, John called people to help prepare a highway through the wilderness, and Jesus comes to take people down this "way of the Lord," where the rough places have been smoothed out and the hills and valleys leveled off. On God's highway we are healed and given new life. Those who have long been silenced now sing God's praises. The blind have all things revealed to them. The deaf hear God's voice. The lame leap for joy.

To know Jesus as Messiah, we must be ready to expect the unexpected. We must be ready for a Messiah who is the hope of all the earth, not just a few "good" people but all people and all of creation. We must expect a Messiah who, though he was "in the form of God," out of love for the world, left God's throne and became a household slave, subject even to death on a cross. His slavery procures our freedom from bondage to sin and death.

Therefore God also highly exalted him
and gave him the name

that is above every name,
so that at the name of Jesus
every knee should bend,
in heaven and on earth and under the earth,
and every tongue should confess
that Jesus Christ is Lord,
to the glory of God the Father. (Philippians 2:9-11)

DAILY SCRIPTURE READINGS

Isaiah 35:1-10; Isaiah 40:1-11; Luke 1:5-25, 57-66; Luke 3:1-20; Isaiah 61:1-4, 8-11; Luke 4:14-29; Malachi 3:1-4; Matthew 11:2-19; Galatians 3:25–4:7; Philippians 2:5-11; Revelation 22:12-21.

PSALM FOR THE WEEK

Read Psalm 85 aloud every day.

HYMN FOR THE WEEK

"Come, Thou Long-Expected Jesus" (*UMH* #196, *NCH* #122, *EH* #66, *PH* #1–2, *LBW* #30, *TBH* #77, *AMECH* #103)

Come, thou long-expected Jesus,
born to set thy people free;
from our fears and sins release us,
let us find our rest in thee.
Israel's strength and consolation,
hope of all the earth thou art;
dear desire of every nation,
joy of every longing heart.
Born thy people to deliver,

born a child and yet a King,
born to reign in us forever,
now thy gracious kingdom bring.
By thine own eternal spirit
rule in all our hearts alone;
by thine all-sufficient merit,
raise us to thy glorious throne.

—CHARLES WESLEY, 1744

This hymn begins by echoing the Maranatha of Revelation 22:20, "Come, Lord Jesus!"—a prayer response used in the early church—and we are reminded again that our Advent prayer for Christ's coming has the double purpose of anticipating the celebration of Jesus' birth in Bethlehem and praying for Christ's return to reign in peace. In the first stanza the hymn writer recognizes Jesus as Savior of Israel, who comes to free his own people in the tradition of Moses and others who worked for God's intervention on behalf of the oppressed. But Jesus is greater than Moses. He is "Israel's strength and consolation" and also "hope of all the earth." Other hymns appropriate to this theme are "Hope of the World" (Georgia Harkness) and "Savior of the Nations, Come" (Martin Luther).

Wesley's words then speak of the freedom Paul declares that each of us enjoys in Christ (Gal. 5:1, 13). The "desire of every nation" is also the "joy of every longing heart," and in our hearts Christ, the only Lord we claim, already rules and frees us from our fears and sins. The hymn also sings of the Incarnation: Christ, who is born as a child and yet is God's royal Son, is both human and divine. Our focus throughout never leaves the theme of Christ's coming reign in an everlasting kingdom that is full of grace.

Day 1

SCRIPTURE

Read aloud Psalm 85.
Read Isaiah 35:1-10 and Isaiah 40:1-11.

IMAGES

Imagine you are on a highway filled with people walking together and singing songs of praise. Describe the highway. Who is with you on that highway?

Imagine what happens when an area of land plagued by drought is suddenly refreshed by streams of water. Relate this image to dry spells in your own life. What has refreshed you?

REFLECTIONS

Reflect on the people named in Isaiah 35:3-6 as being rescued by God. Why did they need God's deliverance? How do fearful hearts (v. 4) make us disabled? Think of recent disasters to the land, both from natural causes and human carelessness. What hope do these verses offer to all people and all of creation? Beginning with Isaiah 35:4, keep a count of the various times during this study we read in the scriptures, "Do not be afraid," associated with God's coming (see also Isa. 40:9).

In what situations do you think the verses we have read from Isaiah 35 and 40 can be used to comfort suffering people? (Examples: funerals, community worship after a disaster.) What was the situation of the people who first heard these words? How did the words speak to the problems of the people who came to Jesus?

PRAYER

Savior, like a shepherd lead us. Care for us tenderly and take us to the still waters of your presence. Free us from all fears; comfort and secure us with your strong arm. Keep us in communion with you and with all the saints, who sing your praises on the highway to your home. In Jesus' name. Amen.

Day 2

SCRIPTURE

Read aloud Psalm 85.
Read Luke 1:5-25, 57-66 and Luke 3:1-20.

IMAGES

Describe what you think the sanctuary of the Temple looked and smelled like with the incense burning and the angel standing at the side of the altar. Describe Zechariah's reaction. Describe the neighbors' reaction to John's birth (Luke 1:66).

Imagine John preaching near Jordan—his dress, his lifestyle, his voice. What about him would cause you to stop and listen?

REFLECTIONS

What stories in the Hebrew Bible should Zechariah have remembered when the angel told him he would become a father in his old age? What do you think Zechariah and Elizabeth taught their son, John, about his religious heritage as he was growing up?

In Luke's version of John's preaching, John tells the people specific injustices that need to be corrected if they truly repent. What are they? (See Luke 3:10-14.) Do you find similar injustices in our society today? Why was Herod angry with John?

PRAYER

Lord God of Israel, you gave us the prophet John to prepare the way of the Lord, and to give knowledge to the people of your forgiveness and salvation. Lead us to the day when, by your tender mercy, the dawn from on high will break upon us to give light to those who sit in darkness and in the shadow of death, to guide our feet into the way of peace. In the name of your Son, Jesus Christ. Amen.[2]

Day 3

SCRIPTURE

Read aloud Psalm 85.
Read Isaiah 61:1-4, 8-11 and Luke 4:14-29.

IMAGES

If you were a movie director, how would you envision a scene leading up to the restoration of Jerusalem by the returned exiles as described in Isaiah 61? How would you show the deprivation the exiles had endured? How would you depict the garland, the oil of gladness, the mantle of praise, and the oaks of righteousness from verse 3?

How would you as a director develop the scene of Jesus' preaching in Nazareth (Luke 4:14-29)? What direction would you give the actors playing the crowd to help them bring alive the scene that leads to the crisis?

Our readings this week include a call to proclaim the gospel or good news (see Isa. 61:1 and 40:9). In Luke 4 Jesus takes this as his own calling. Reflect on the calling you received at your baptism. What is the good news God wants us to proclaim? How can we proclaim good news to the poor and oppressed? Whose "broken hearts" are we expected to bind (Isa. 61:1)?

"The year of the Lord's favor," mentioned in Isaiah 61:2 and Luke 4:19, recalls the Jubilee Year, a sabbatical year when debts are canceled, slaves are freed, liberty is proclaimed for all, and the land is restored (see Lev. 25). What do these ancient traditions tell us about the characteristics of Christ's coming reign and what we should be doing to work for that reign now? Why do you think it is true that "no prophet is accepted in the prophet's hometown" (Luke 4:24)?

PRAYER

Holy God, you have called us to follow Jesus. Give us his compassion for those who need healing and those who want to be freed. Help us seek your justice for all so that we may live in your favor. Prepare us to find in the coming celebration of Christmas a new invitation to live in your reign now. In the name of your Son, who reigns with you and the Holy Spirit, now and forever. Amen.

Day 4

SCRIPTURE

Read aloud Psalm 85.
Read Malachi 3:1-4 and Matthew 11:2-19.

IMAGES

Imagine a child making a Christmas wish list. How does he or she decide what to include? Are the expectations realistic? How do we teach children—children all over the world in all sorts of situations—what to expect at Christmas?

Imagine the kind of Christmas celebration you expect to have. Imagine the ways you expect to welcome Jesus into your life, now and in the future.

REFLECTIONS

Why has Malachi 3:1-4 traditionally been associated with John the Baptist? For whom was John's preaching good news and for whom was it bad news? Why were Jesus and John executed?

What did the crowds to whom Jesus spoke in Matthew 11:7-19 find surprising and even disturbing about Jesus? What deeds of Jesus proved his wisdom (v. 19)? If Advent is a time of waiting and expectation, what do the readings in Malachi and Matthew suggest we should expect?

PRAYER

Come, thou long-expected Jesus. Bring joy to longing hearts, strength and consolation to those who wait, and hope to all the earth. Come, O unexpected Jesus. Come in ways we never anticipated. Teach us what to hope for; give us the patience and energy to work for your reign now. Free us from all fear, for to you belong all honor and glory, now and forever. Amen.

Day 5

SCRIPTURE

Read aloud Psalm 85.
Read Galatians 3:25–4:7 and the hymn "Come, Thou Long-Expected Jesus."

IMAGES

Another Wesley hymn, "And Can It Be That I Should Gain" (*UMH* #363, *TBH* #147) expresses the freedom each of us obtains from Christ, using images from the stories of Peter in Acts 12 and Paul in Acts 16:

> Long my imprisoned spirit lay,
> fast bound in sin and nature's night;
> thine eye diffused a quickening ray;
> I woke, the dungeon flamed with light;
> my chains fell off, my heart was free,
> I rose, went forth and followed thee.

Using these or other images, think about how you experience freedom from the coming of Jesus to you now. Think of someone to pray for who needs the freedom Jesus brings.

According to "Come, Thou Long-Expected Jesus" (p. 31), from what does Jesus free us? Why is the release of captives a powerful image in both Testaments? Why does freedom in Christ make us "new creations"?

What is the significance of Paul's telling the Galatians that through Christ they became God's children and off-spring of Abraham (3:26-29)? How have you been changed by being "clothed . . . with Christ" in baptism (v. 27)? Reflect on the implications for individuals and for churches of this statement: God has accepted and adopted us; therefore, we are God's children and heirs, no longer slaves (4:6-7).

PRAYER

God of freedom, we give you thanks for Jesus, who came as a slave to set us free. We thank you that you call us your children. By your Spirit of freedom, help us to love all our sisters and brothers. Free us to work for your justice, live lives pleasing to you, and join with all the saints in your reign of peace. In Jesus' name. Amen.

Day 6

SCRIPTURE

Read aloud Psalm 85.
Read Philippians 2:5-11 and Revelation 22:12-21.

IMAGES

Think of Jesus' birth in a stable. Why was he born like a slave instead of like a king? Remember Jesus' Palm Sunday ride into Jerusalem. What in this scene shows Jesus' humility? What images of kingship accompany Jesus' ride?

Think of Jesus washing the disciples' feet before the Crucifixion (John 13:3-15) and cooking their breakfast after the Resurrection (John 21:9-13). Describe the disciples' reaction to these examples of Jesus serving them like a household slave.

REFLECTIONS

What does Philippians 2:5-11 say about the reason for Jesus' leaving God's throne and coming as a servant/savior? What do we learn about Jesus' divinity and his humanity from these verses? Who does this ancient hymn tell us Jesus is?

Though many readers have tried with little success to tie Revelation's warnings to specific current events, only one certainty is asserted in Revelation 22:12-21. What certainty about our future can we affirm from these verses? Why does his promised return cause us to be hopeful? What do you think about when you pray, "Come, Lord Jesus"?

PRAYER

Come, Lord Jesus! Pitch your tent and make your home with us. Be our friend and helper every day. Open our ears to your teachings, and strengthen us for the tasks you have given us. Come to reign in our hearts now, and come at last to reign in all the world. We praise your name and bow before you, for you are Jesus Christ, the Lord of heaven and earth. Amen.

Third Week of Advent

❦

EXPECTING THE JOY OF HEAVEN

"Do not be afraid, Mary, for you have found favor with God.
And now, you will conceive in your womb and bear a son,
and you will name him Jesus."

— LUKE 1:30-31

Jesus is the joy of heaven; his coming to earth is "good news of great joy for all the people" (Luke 2:10). Jesus tells the disciples that when he returns, no one will take their joy from them (John 16:22). Jesus is all compassion—God's unbounded love that excels all other loves. Jesus is like no other. In leading us to this conclusion, the story we read in the Bible that begins "Now the birth of Jesus the Messiah took place in this way" (Matt. 1:18) pulls out all the stops, employs every poetic device, and entices us with references to older stories of God's marvelous deeds. In Luke we find breathtaking arias sung by Zechariah, Mary, and Simeon. In Matthew and Luke we see angelic appearances—God's messenger startling the recipients with news from God. The birth that takes place will strike fear in the hearts of the treacherous and bring good news to the poor and the outcast.

The Annunciation story in Luke has been a favorite subject of art for hundreds of years. The artists of each generation have placed the event described in Luke 1:26-38 in their own time. Mary often is shown in a room and in clothing of the artist's own era. We have done somewhat the same thing by trying to make of Mary, Joseph, and the child Jesus an ideal contemporary nuclear family. Sometimes we see them as if through a soft-focus lens, wrapped in a hazy mantle of wishful thinking about the way we would like to be. For many among us—for families in crisis, for individuals who feel lonely or abandoned, and for those who have chosen to live outside the conventional family norm—such an idealization of family can be painful.

The biblical story, however, won't let us become sentimental about Mary and Joseph. They don't fit easily into a modern middle-class family model. Luke's Gospel emphasizes the historical and political constraints on their lives. They lived in a poor country under foreign domination, subject to Rome's whims. They were forced by Caesar's tax census to travel a long distance at the time of Mary's delivery. The story in Matthew shows that they risked being ostracized by their own community because of the unexpected nature of Mary's pregnancy, and they endured homelessness in both Gospel accounts. There was no place for them in Roman-occupied Bethlehem on the night of Jesus' birth (Luke 2:7), and while Jesus was still a baby, they were warned to flee and live like refugees in Egypt because of Herod's treachery (Matt. 2:13).

Another problem that misleading interpretations of the biblical story presents is based on Mary's declaration, "Here am I, the servant of the Lord" (Luke 1:38). This statement has been used at times by authorities to encourage women to see themselves as servants and thus subservient to men. This misuse of the Annunciation story completely conflicts with the Bible's intent. We should see Mary's statement instead as an indication of her place of honor as the one chosen to play a key role in God's plan for bringing newness and life to the world. Her words echo Jesus' own in Luke 22:27: " 'I am among you as one who serves,' " and Matthew 20:26: " 'Whoever wishes to be great among you must be your servant.' " Jesus came as a household slave (Phil. 2:7)—the Greek word *doulos* here translated "slave" is the same word translated "servant" in Luke 1:38—and God exalted him. We are called, women and men together, to be like Jesus.

The biblical story won't let us become sentimental about Mary and Jesus. They don't fit easily into a modern middle-class family model.

Mary's song of liberation in Luke 1:46-55 follows closely the pattern of women's songs in the Hebrew Bible: Miriam (Exod. 15:20-21), Hannah (1 Sam. 2:1-10), and in the Apocrypha, Judith (Judith 16:1-17). Miriam is called a prophet, and her namesake Mary fulfills this role too. Through the power of the Holy Spirit, Mary sees in the birth of her Son the beginning of God's plan for changing the world into a place where the lowly are lifted up, the mighty toppled from their thrones, the poor filled with good things, the rich sent away empty, and the proud scattered by God's might alone. These words echo Isaiah's poetic prophecy of God's great reversal, the beginning of God's just and peaceable reign.

Joseph, the often-neglected character in the birth drama, is an intriguing figure. His love and respect for Mary are obvious, and his devotion to God's word is a blessing for us all. God asks him to do two very odd things: (1) he must accept Mary's pregnancy as the work of the Holy Spirit, marry her, and raise the child; (2) after the visit of the magi, he is told to flee by night with Mary and the child and remain in Egypt until Herod dies. We need Joseph's courage and willing spirit to face the risks we are asked to take and the strange things are we called to do as God's servants.

The hardest conundrum for modern readers, of course, is the story of the miraculous conception itself. We regard ourselves as intelligent Christians who are aware of the significance of this belief for our ancestors, but for moderns who know a thing or two about reproductive biology, repeating the phrase in the Apostles' Creed, "born of the Virgin Mary," may require some suspension of doubt. Scholars point to a textual problem here. The prophecy from Isaiah 7:14 on which this description of Mary is based is translated in the NRSV as "Look, the young woman is with child," but in the Septuagint, the Greek translation of the Hebrew Bible that the New Testament writers knew, "young woman" becomes "virgin." Either translation is possible from the Hebrew. The quibbling over translation, however, is beside the point. The intent of the biblical account is to point to God's power for life at work, and the Gospel writers are more interested in poetry than in biology. The truth of the poetry is clear: Mary and Joseph were to expect a miraculous birth—Jesus, born of a woman, would be the true Son of God.

The young woman about to give birth in Isaiah 7:14 was God's sign for King Ahaz, meant to encourage him to trust

The hardest conundrum for modern readers is the story of the miraculous conception itself.

God and rely on God's presence and power rather than on his own military might. Mary's pregnancy is God's sign of hope for all times, and Gabriel's response to Mary's puzzlement helps us see the significance of the sign: with God nothing is impossible. Her cousin Elizabeth recognized the sign immediately and blessed Mary for believing "that there would be a fulfillment of what was spoken to her by the Lord" (Luke 2:45). God's promises are true, and God is faithful. God does the unexpected in order to save us and set us free.

Mary's pregnancy is God's sign of hope for all times.

The Gospel accounts of the Annunciation to Mary (Luke) and to Joseph (Matthew) point to the uniqueness of Jesus' birth even as the stories remind us that we have knowledge from the past of God's power to bring life out of hopeless situations. Isaac, Samuel, and John the Baptist were all born after God's intervention. The son Obed born to Ruth and Boaz, who was, indeed, King David's grandfather and therefore Jesus' ancestor, was known as a "restorer of life" (Ruth 4:15) because he was born to a family that was as good as dead. God always acts to restore the life of the community.

God responds with these words to Sarah after she has laughed at the idea that she will become a mother in her old age: "Is anything too wonderful for the LORD?" (Gen. 18:14). Gabriel says much the same thing to Mary in Luke 1:37: "Nothing will be impossible with God." And Mary has the last word with her affirmation of God's power: "The Mighty One has done great things for me, and holy is his name" (Luke 1:49).

DAILY SCRIPTURE READINGS

Matthew 1:1-17; Colossians 1:11-20; Isaiah 7:10-16; Matthew 1:18-25; Luke 1:26-45; Micah 5:2-5; Luke 1:67-80;

Isaiah 57:14-19; 1 Thessalonians 5:12-24; Luke 2:22-38; Romans 1:1-7

Read Mary's Song, Luke 1:46-55, aloud every day. (The Bible contains many songs or canticles in addition to the Psalms. This one is the most well-known and has been used in Christian worship throughout church history.)

> My soul proclaims the greatness of the Lord,
> my spirit rejoices in God my Savior,
> who has looked with favor on me, a lowly servant.
> From this day all generations shall call me blessed:
> the Almighty has done great things for me
> and holy is the name of the Lord,
> whose mercy is on those who fear God
> from generation to generation.
> The arm of the Lord is strong,
> and has scattered the proud in their conceit.
> God has cast down the mighty from their thrones
> and lifted up the lowly.
> God has filled the hungry with good things
> and sent the rich empty away.
> God has come to the aid of Israel, the chosen servant,
> remembering the promise of mercy,
> the promise made to our forebears,
> to Abraham and his children for ever. (Luke 1:46-55)

English translation of the Canticle of Mary, © English Language Liturgical Consultation (ELLC), 1998 and used by permission. See www.englishtexts.com.

"Love Divine, All Loves Excelling" (*UMH #384, NCH #43, EH #657, PH #376, LBW #315, AMECH #455, TBH #208*)

Love divine, all loves excelling,
joy of heaven, to earth come down;
fix in us thy humble dwelling;
all thy faithful mercies crown!
Jesus, thou art all compassion,
pure, unbounded love thou art;
visit us with thy salvation;
enter every trembling heart.

Breathe, O breathe thy loving Spirit
into every troubled breast!
Let us all in thee inherit;
let us find that second rest.
Take away our bent to sinning;
Alpha and Omega be;
end of faith, as its beginning,
set our hearts at liberty.

Come, Almighty, to deliver,
let us all thy life receive;
suddenly return and never,
nevermore thy temples leave.
Thee we would be always blessing,
serve thee as thy hosts above,
pray and praise thee without ceasing,
glory in thy perfect love.

Finish, then, thy new creation;
pure and spotless let us be.

Let us see thy great salvation
perfectly restored in thee;
changed from glory into glory,
till in heaven we take our place,
till we cast our crowns before thee,
lost in wonder, love, and praise.

—CHARLES WESLEY, 1747

The first two stanzas of this hymn address Jesus, and the last two address Almighty God, though the unity of the song makes clear that praying for God's coming and for Jesus' coming are the same thing. The Trinitarian focus is completed with a reference to the work of the Spirit in stanza 2. This is another Wesley hymn appropriate for the Advent season, as well as for other occasions that relate to the return and reign of Christ. The text of "Love Divine, All Loves Excelling" has similarities to "Come, Thou Long-Expected Jesus," and they can be sung to the same tunes. The second stanza refers to our inheritance through Christ, Galatians 4:6-7: "God has sent the Spirit of his Son into our hearts, . . . and if a child then also an heir," and to Revelation 22:13: "I am the Alpha and the Omega."

The images in this hymn are often astounding in their complex allusions. "Thy humble dwelling," for example, brings to mind the stable, the image from John 1:14 of the Word pitching a tent to live among us, and Revelation 21:3: "'See, the home of God is among mortals.'" It is also intended to remind us that Christ's "humble dwelling" is our own "trembling hearts" (Isa. 57:15). An important aspect of this hymn is its call to our vocation in Christ's reign: we are to bless and serve, to "pray and praise thee without ceasing, glory in thy perfect love" (1 Thess. 5:16). And finally, before God's throne, we are "lost in wonder, love, and praise." The catechism we learned as children declared a similar purpose: Our chief end is to glorify God and enjoy God forever. The final stanza brings us back to our focus in chapter 1: "Finish, then, thy new creation." As Advent people, even in the distress and distractions of our imperfect times on earth, we can count on God entering our lives and restoring us, making us new and holy, set apart for God's work—blessing, serving, and praising.

Day 1

SCRIPTURE

Read aloud Mary's Song, Luke 1:46-55.
Read Matthew 1:1-17 and Colossians 1:11-20.

IMAGES

Focus on a tree in your yard, in a picture, or in your imagination. What associations come to mind? Think of the tree in the garden of Eden, the tree of life with healing leaves in Revelation 22:2, a family tree—yours and Jesus'—and a Christmas tree.

Imagine a gathering of the "saints in the light" (Col. 1:12). Where are they and what are they doing? What do we inherit from them? Do you know any of the saints in this gathering?

REFLECTIONS

Five women have a place in Jesus' genealogy in Matthew 1:1-17: Tamar, Rahab, Ruth, the wife of Uriah (Bathsheba), and Mary. Each one is an unexpected candidate to be honored as an ancestor of Jesus. Ruth, for example, was a foreigner. Look up the passages about these women, or recall what you know about their stories. Why do you think God chose them for this honor? What does this genealogy say about who Jesus is?

What does Colossians 1:11-20 say about Jesus' divinity? What do these verses tell us about God's plan to reconcile God and creation? List the roles of Jesus Christ mentioned in these verses and think about each one (example: "firstborn from the dead," v. 18).

PRAYER

Loving God, you have reconciled us to yourself through your Son's death and resurrection. Strengthen us with your glorious power, and prepare us to welcome Jesus joyfully into our lives again. Help us be good citizens of your reign, offering mercy and kindness in your name. We give you thanks and praise. In Jesus' name. Amen.

Day 2

SCRIPTURE

Read aloud Mary's Song, Luke 1:46-55.
Read Isaiah 7:10-16 and Matthew 1:18-25.

IMAGES

The image of a woman joyfully expecting a baby is easily seen as a sign of hope. What other signs can we find around us that help us remember and trust God's promises?

Imagine how Joseph felt when he first heard of Mary's pregnancy. What character traits helped him through this difficult predicament? What practices and habits do you imagine he relied upon? Which of these were related to his faith?

REFLECTIONS

Why are we sometimes reluctant, like King Ahaz in Isaiah 7:10-16, to accept the signs God gives us? Which do you think concerned Ahaz the most: keeping the commandment against putting God to the test, or the fear that he might lose his control by putting his kingdom's security in God's hand? What do we give up when we put our faith completely in God's power? What do we gain?

What makes Jesus' birth different from that of any of his ancestors, including Isaac? What signs does Matthew give that Jesus comes from God and will do God's work? What two names for the Messiah are found in Matthew 1:18-25, and what do they mean?

PRAYER

Faithful God, you have shown us the rainbow in the clouds, the streams in the desert, and the child of hope. Take away our doubts and fears. Give us the assurance of your strong and loving arms. Be with us in our troubles and in our joy. O come, O come, Emmanuel. Amen.

Day 3

SCRIPTURE

Read aloud Mary's Song, Luke 1:46-55.
Read Luke 1:26-45.

IMAGES

The image of a pregnant woman is seen as a sign of hope and expectancy, but some situations make an impending birth difficult to anticipate without fear. What conditions make hopefulness possible when a new child comes into the world? What experiences in your life have made you watchful and hopeful for a new beginning?

Imagine Mary and Elizabeth's meeting. What do you think they talked about? Laughed about? What do you think each of them may have feared? Remember a friend in your life—maybe someone older or younger than you—with whom you can share your deepest thoughts and feelings.

REFLECTIONS

Why is Mary called "favored one" (Luke 1:28)? What other words could be used in Gabriel's greeting to bring out all the possible meanings of having God's favor (examples: "chosen one," "grace-filled one")? Why does Gabriel tell her not to be afraid? What qualities are needed to respond to God's call the way Mary did (v. 38)?

In Luke 1:46-55, Mary addresses God as "my Savior." What does "Savior" mean? In verses 50-53, what is God saving the people from? Who in Luke's story recognizes their need for God's salvation and who does not?

PRAYER

Merciful God, you have favored us with your grace and given us reason to expect your coming. Help us believe in the fulfillment of your word and live in hope. Wake us up to the needs of the weak and the hungry. Free us from our pride and fear. In the name of your Son, Jesus Christ. Amen.

Day 4

SCRIPTURE

Read aloud Mary's Song, Luke 1:46-55.
Read Micah 5:2-5 and Luke 1:67-80.

IMAGES

Jesus is called "dayspring," "the bright and morning star."
Zechariah speaks of Jesus' coming as the "dawn from on
high" that "will break upon us." Think of a dawn in your life
that has saved you from despair or fear (Luke 1:67-80). Think
of Advent candles as signs that point to the coming dawn.

What comes to your mind when you think of those who
are "in the shadow of death"? In what sense do we all live in
the shadow of death today? How do you picture the coming
of Jesus to give us light? In what direction does the light of
Jesus guide us (v. 79)?

REFLECTIONS

Look for clues in Zechariah's Song (Luke 1:68-79) that connect Jesus' birth to the prophets of old and God's saving
works among the Hebrew people. What does Zechariah say
directly to the child John? How can we as a faithful congregation help children have a sense of their calling to serve God?

What about Bethlehem makes its choice as the birthplace
of the Anointed One a sign of God's great reversal (Mic.
5:2)? What do you read in verse 3 that recalls God's inten-
tion to restore the life of the community? What are the
attributes of the just ruler described in verses 4-5?

PRAYER

God, our light and our salvation, you have spoken through the prophets of old, and you have shown mercy to our ancestors. Rescue us now from our enemies—from all those things that keep us from trusting in you completely—and help us serve you without fear. Prepare us for the coming of the dawn so we may stand not in shadows but in your glorious light. In Jesus' name. Amen.

Day 5

SCRIPTURE

Read aloud Mary's Song, Luke 1:46-55.
Read Isaiah 57:14-19 and 1 Thessalonians 5:12-24.
Read the hymn "Love Divine, All Loves Excelling."

IMAGES

Picture in your mind God's dwelling places that are alluded to in Isaiah 57:15. How are both concepts of where God lives represented in "Love Divine, All Loves Excelling"? What two contrasting pictures of God do you find in Isaiah 57:17-18?

REFLECTIONS

In what ways are we called today to "build," "prepare," and "remove every obstruction" (Isa. 57:14)? What tasks are given to us in 1 Thessalonians 5:12-24 and in Charles Wesley's hymn?

How can we pray and praise "without ceasing" (1 Thess. 5:17; "Love Divine, All Loves Excelling," stanza 3)? What do we mean when we pray to be kept "blameless" (v. 23) or "spotless" ("Love Divine, All Loves Excelling," stanza 4) "at the coming of our Lord Jesus Christ"? Who will do this for us (v. 24; stanza 4)? What do we mean when we pray for God to "finish, then, thy new creation"?

PRAYER

Mighty God, you have told us to rejoice always, seek to do good to one another, and be at peace. Help us rely on your strength and faithfulness in all things. Breathe your loving Spirit into us; calm us and give us words to praise you in wonder, for you have done marvelous things for us. We give you thanks through Jesus Christ our Lord. Amen.

Day 6

SCRIPTURE

Read aloud Mary's Song, Luke 1:46-55.
Read Luke 2:22-38 and Romans 1:1-7.

IMAGES

In Luke 2:22-38 we read of the response to the infant Jesus by two faithful people in the Temple. Picture the scene with Simeon, a respected elder, and Anna, a poor widow, rejoicing over the birth of the Messiah. What thoughts run through your head when you see or hold a new baby? What had God revealed to Simeon and Anna about this child?

Both Paul (Rom. 1:3) and John's Gospel (John 1:14) use the word *flesh* to refer to Jesus' physical nature. What comes to mind when you hear the word *flesh*? Why do you think the writers chose this word instead of a more elegant term for Jesus' bodily existence?

REFLECTIONS

In what ways do Simeon's words connect the Gospel stories of Jesus' birth and his crucifixion and resurrection? What do you think Mary felt on hearing Simeon's warning addressed to her (Luke 2:34-35)?

For Paul writing in Romans 1:1-7, what is the most significant indication that Jesus is God's Son? What evidence does he cite of Jesus' humanity? Reflect on the way Paul talks about the wholeness of the story from the prophets to the Resurrection. What does this story mean for us, according to verses 5-6?

PRAYER

God of grace and peace, you have called us to belong to Jesus Christ. Guide us by your Spirit to speak of him with joy and live always in the circle of his love. Teach us to rejoice like Anna and Simeon at the coming of your Son and to recognize him as the Anointed One of God. For the sake of Jesus' name. Amen.

Fourth Week of Advent

❧

EXPECTING THE SUN OF RIGHTEOUSNESS

"Do not be afraid; for see—I am bringing you good news of great joy for all the people: to you is born this day in the city of David a Savior, who is the Messiah, the Lord."
— LUKE 2:10-11

Shepherds are a recurring theme in the Bible. Abraham was a nomadic shepherd, a rich man with servants and many flocks, but nevertheless a shepherd who lived in a tent where he received God as a guest. Abraham and Sarah's descendants were shepherds until Joseph was appointed Pharaoh's prime minister and brought his family to Egypt, where they eventually became slaves. The people, multiplied into a nation, finally returned to freedom and shepherding, led by Moses, who left his life as a shepherd of his father-in-law's flocks and became the shepherd of God's people. David was the great shepherd king of Israel; God instructed Samuel to bring him in from the fields and anoint him. Some of God's prophets also were shepherds. Amos identifies himself as one of the "shepherds of Tekoa" (Amos 1:1). There are evil shepherds too, and they are often blamed for Israel's falling away from God's word. The prophet Ezekiel speaks God's judgment against the shepherds/rulers who failed to care for God's people (Ezek. 34:1-10). It's no wonder the biblical image of a good leader is of one who knows how to be a good shepherd.

The shepherds on the hills near Bethlehem must have inherited some of the ancient shepherds' mystique. Like David who slew the bear and the lion to protect his sheep, they wore the mantle of good protectors. They also played a significant role in the economy of their poor country. Shepherds, often the pipeline of news for the community, were usually the first to hear the heralds on the mountaintops, sent from the authorities to spread important announcements throughout the countryside. Thus shepherds probably were a good source for underground news as well. They were not idyllic, carefree pastoral figures, however, and probably were not on the preferred list of desirable dinner guests in town; Luke tells us they lived in the fields (2:8). Shepherds were just the kind of persons Jesus sought out, and they were the first to hear the news of his birth. Luke's shepherds, who knew hardship and carried the news of Rome's insufferable edicts, were remarkably responsive to the angel's message. They found what they were looking for—a sign from God that this baby, swaddled and lying in the manger, was indeed God's "good shepherd [who] lays down his life for the sheep" (John 10:11).

In Luke's Christmas story, a stable at the end of a journey,

The shepherds on the hills near Bethlehem must have inherited some of the ancient shepherds' mystique.

smelling of hay and animals, becomes the birthplace of a baby who was visited first by rough shepherds. What does this tell us? That Jesus came to human beings in all our inadequacy and with all our problems. Yet more than this, he came to be one of us, taking on our weakness, born to a family with few possibilities and therefore leaning on God's promises for a future; born to a people who longed for God's reign without end. The poem of the Incarnation in John 1:1-14 offers another way to express this remarkable coming of God to live with the people and become one of them: "The Word became flesh and lived among us, and we have seen his glory, the glory of a father's only son, full of grace and truth" (v. 14). "Hark! the Herald Angels Sing" tells us that Jesus came as the Godhead made visible in the humanity of Jesus: "Veiled in flesh the Godhead see; . . . pleased with us in flesh to dwell, Jesus, our Emmanuel."

The idea that God would come to live with us is not a new one.

The idea that God would come to live with us is not a new one. Early in Exodus, God speaks to Moses from the bush: " 'I have observed the misery of my people. . . . I have heard their cry. . . . Indeed, I know their sufferings, and I have come down to deliver them from the Egyptians, and to bring them up out of that land to a good and broad land, a land flowing with milk and honey' " (Exod. 3:7-8). And in 2 Samuel 7:1-13 God tells the prophet Nathan that David doesn't need to build a grand temple because God prefers to live in a tent that can be moved about wherever God's people go. God is aware of our suffering; God is willing to respond to our cries and walk with us. Moses already knows this when he asks God's name. Moses asks, "What shall I tell the people your name is?" God replies to Moses, "I am who I am," (Exod. 3:13-15), a name that carries with it a story, a history, of God being with us. Moses already knows God as Emmanuel.

What is new about the Christmas story is *Jesus.* In Jesus God is doing a completely new thing, something amazing and truly unthinkable. In Jesus God comes as a baby—helpless, hungry, and subject to pain—a baby who will grow up to be a teacher, healer, friend, and servant of all, and who will one day suffer and die to free all humanity from sin and death. What wondrous love is this!

The end of the story is already visible in the story of the birth and the many ways we are told who this baby is—the prophecy of Zechariah, the pondering of Mary, the warning of Simeon. Luke's Gospel contains parallel verses in its birth and crucifixion narratives that show us where the story is leading: " 'This will be a sign for you: you will find a child wrapped in bands of cloth and lying in a manger' " (2:12); and "This man [Joseph of Arimathea] went to Pilate and asked for the body of Jesus. Then he took it down, wrapped it in a linen cloth, and laid it in a rock-hewn tomb" (23:52-53). The bands of cloth are a sign for us as well as for the shepherds: they serve as swaddling for the newborn baby and a shroud for the crucified Jesus.

The Crucifixion is not the end either, of course; if it were, we could not sing the last stanza of "Hark! the Herald Angels Sing." We can't celebrate Christmas as if the cute baby pictured on the cards we receive never grew up, and we can't celebrate if we see only the shadow of the Cross over the cradle. We celebrate Christmas around an empty manger, an empty cross, and an empty tomb. We celebrate Jesus Christ, Son of God; born of Mary; baptized by John; anointed by the Holy Spirit to bring good news to the poor; crucified, dead, and buried; raised by God on the third day; and exalted to reign with God and the Holy Spirit, one God now and forever. We celebrate Jesus, the One who came and the Coming One. The miraculous birth of Jesus to a poor family in a dying land is a foretaste of the miracle of the Resurrection; both are the result of God's power to bring life out of death, God's power that is available to us now.

In recent years some religious leaders have objected to the use in popular culture of "Happy Holidays" as a greeting instead of "Merry Christmas." I have thought that perhaps "Merry Christmas" as a greeting that truly rejoices in the coming of Jesus, is an inadequate choice as well. I'm not convinced it really matters what television personalities say in greeting; most of what we hear on commercial channels is designed to support the shopping season rather than the religious holiday. But for those of us in the community of Jesus Christ, it does matter how we greet each other.

We celebrate Jesus, the One who came and the Coming One.

"Merry" and "Christmas" are a strange combination. "Christmas" is a fine word, coming from Christ Mass, meaning the celebration of the Eucharist—the grace of God in the free gift of Jesus Christ—on Christmas Day. Mass is a solemn occasion whenever it is celebrated because it commemorates at all times of the year the death and resurrection of Jesus Christ. "Merry," on the other hand, brings to mind a kind of thoughtless reveling. Jesus spoke against an "eat-drink-and-be-merry" attitude toward life (Luke 12:19-21).

We find excellent Christmas greetings in the hymns we sing—"Good Christian Friends, Rejoice," for example, and "Joy to the World." From our hymn for this week, "Hark! the Herald Angels Sing," we find "Peace" as a greeting: "Peace on earth, and mercy mild"; and "Joy" in the angels' song: "Glory to the newborn King!" These hymns and many others in the Christmas section of our hymnals understand the full story of the Christ Mass and do not leave out, in the midst of celebrating the birth story, the remembrance of Jesus' life-giving death on the Cross. As you sing carols this season, look for references to Jesus' death and resurrection, especially in the second, third, and fourth stanzas.

The very first Christmas greeting, given by the angel to the shepherds, was "Do not be afraid." This greeting from God always precedes an announcement of God's presence and has ancient Hebrew origins. It may be the greeting we most need to hear today to confront the multitude of fears—terrorism, various disasters around the world, family problems, personal indebtedness, illness, troubles of every kind—that enter our lives. "Do not worry about anything, but in everything by prayer and supplication with thanksgiving let your requests be made known to God. And the peace of God, which surpasses all understanding, will guard your hearts and your minds in Christ Jesus" (Phil. 4:6-7). Merriness may seem out of place at Christmas in these troubled times, but joy is expected. "The shepherds returned, glorifying and praising God for all they had heard and seen" (Luke 2:20).

The very first Christmas greeting was "Do not be afraid."

How can we not be joyful when our Lord has come? "Rejoice in the Lord always; again I will say, Rejoice. . . . The Lord is near" (Phil. 4:4-5).

DAILY SCRIPTURE READINGS

Isaiah 43:1-7; Philippians 4:4-7; Exodus 3:1-15; Hebrews 1:1-13; Isaiah 52:7-10; Luke 2:1-20; 2 Samuel 7:1-13; John 1:1-14; John 3:1-17; Romans 5:8-11; Isaiah 9:2-7; Titus 3:4-7

Read Psalm 98 aloud every day.

"Hark! the Herald Angels Sing" (*UMH* #240, *NCH* #160, *EH* #87, *PH* #31, *LBW* #60, *AMECH* #115, *TBH* #88)

Hark! the herald angels sing, "Glory to the newborn King;
peace on earth, and mercy mild, God and sinners reconciled!"
Joyful, all ye nations rise, join the triumph of the skies;
with th' angelic host proclaim, "Christ is born in Bethlehem!"
Hark! the herald angels sing, "Glory to the newborn King!"

Christ, by highest heaven adored; Christ, the everlasting Lord;
late in time behold him come, offspring of a virgin's womb.
Veiled in flesh the Godhead see; hail th' incarnate Deity,
pleased with us in flesh to dwell, Jesus, our Emmanuel.
Hark! the herald angels sing, "Glory to the newborn King!"

Hail the heaven-born Prince of Peace! Hail the Sun of Righteousness!
Light and life to all he brings, risen with healing in his wings.
Mild he lays his glory by, born that we no more may die,
born to raise us from the earth, born to give us second birth.
Hark! the herald angels sing, "Glory to the newborn King!"
—CHARLES WESLEY, 1739

This hymn begins with the refrain the angels sing to the shepherds. God's own angel messengers are the heralds on the mountaintops who bring good news (Isa. 52:7). Peace on earth in line 2 is joined to God's mercy and God's reconciliation with us sinners (Rom. 5:8-11). As in the Prophets (Isa. 2:1-3, for example), all the nations rise to join the heavenly hosts in proclaiming God's salvation.

The second stanza contains a remarkable articulation of the Incarnation: Christ, adored by heaven, comes to earth as the son of a virgin. Thus clothed in flesh, Jesus makes the invisible Godhead visible. The veil suggests the story of Moses, coming off the mountain after spending time with God face-to-face. Moses must veil his own face, which is shining with God's glory, because the people are afraid to look directly at him (Exod. 34:33-35). In Jesus we all can see God face-to-face. Jesus is pleased to live with us—our Emmanuel.

Nearly every phrase in stanza 3 has a biblical reference. The title Prince of Peace comes from Isaiah 9:6. The image of the Messiah as the Sun of Righteousness risen with healing wings is from Malachi 4:2. "Light and life to all he brings" echoes John 1:3-4. Lines 3 and 4 of stanza 3 remind us of Philippians 2:6-8 with allusions to 1 Corinthians 15:51-52 and John 3:7. The whole story of Jesus' birth, death, and resurrection is reviewed in this Christmas hymn, and we begin to see what "the newborn King" will do for the world.

Day 7

SCRIPTURE

Read Psalm 98 aloud.
Read Isaiah 43:1-7 and Philippians 4:4-7.

IMAGES

Imagine yourself in the community to whom Isaiah 43:1-2 is addressed. Remember a difficult time you have experienced in your life. Do you think of this trouble as water or fire? Did you feel you were being overwhelmed or consumed? Pray that you will always know God's presence. Pray that you will hear God call your name.

Think of a Christmas celebration that is a reunion of family and close friends. Imagine the people you love coming from north, south, east, and west as in Isaiah 43:5-7. Think of the joy to be shared and the tears to be shed. Remember that joyful gatherings at Christmas feasts are a foretaste of God's heavenly banquet, and give thanks.

REFLECTIONS

In Isaiah 43, verse 1 says, "Do not fear, for I have redeemed you," and verse 5 says, "Do not fear, for I am with you." What does each verse say to you? What does God's knowing our name have to do with our redemption? Why are these verses often used at baptisms?

Philippians 4:4-7 tells us not to worry but to pray, to let our "gentleness be known," and to rejoice. Reflect on the ways we can follow Paul's admonitions throughout the Christmas season and beyond. What reason does Paul give us for not worrying and instead rejoicing? What do you think Paul means by the "peace of God"?

PRAYER

God of hope and joy, you have promised to go with us through all our troubled times. Help us to lay aside our fears and worries; give us grace to lean on you, for you are with us. Teach us to treat others with your gentle kindness and to rejoice in your gift of Jesus Christ, in whose name we pray. Amen.

Day 2

SCRIPTURE

Read Psalm 98 aloud.
Read Exodus 3:1-15 and Hebrews 1:1-13.

IMAGES

In your mind narrate a story God might tell you about your ancestors that shows how God has been present with your people always. Choose a story about either your family ancestors or your faith ancestors from the Bible. What other images from Bible stories give you reassurance and hope for the future?

Imagine the angels described in Hebrews 1:7. What is their job? Are they like the Christmas angels in your imagination? This verse quotes Psalm 104:4 and has similar imagery to the story of the coming of the Holy Spirit in Acts 2. Spend some time thinking about wind, water, and fire in these references and in Isaiah 43:2 and how they are associated throughout the Bible with God's coming.

REFLECTIONS

What does God's conversation with Moses in Exodus 3:1-15 tell us about God's feelings toward humanity and God's desire to be with us? What stories about God's relationship with Moses' ancestors are alluded to in these verses? To what event in Moses' future does the sign in verse 12 refer?

What does Hebrews 1:1-13 tell us about Christ's origins? How did the Son make "purification for sins" (v. 3)? Verse

13 quotes Psalm 110:1, as do Acts 2:34-35 and 1 Corinthians 15:25-26. Why do you think this verse was so important for early Christians?

PRAYER

God of our ancestors, you spoke through the prophets, and you speak to us through your Son. Open our ears to your words and our hearts to the coming of your Word made flesh. Help us to see your glory reflected in Jesus and to know him as "the imprint of your very being." We give you thanks for your presence with our ancestors and with us. In Jesus' name. Amen.

Day 3

SCRIPTURE

Read Psalm 98 aloud.
Read Isaiah 52:7-10 and Luke 2:1-20.

IMAGES

Imagine you are one of the sentinels in Isaiah 52:8, and you are looking for the messenger on the mountains. What can you tell from the messenger's feet? What announcement do you hear? Who are heralds of peace today?

New mothers often keep baby books or photo albums. How did Mary save her memories? What images do you think she treasured the most?

REFLECTIONS

Why is the announcement that God reigns in Isaiah 52:7 good news to the exiles returned from Babylon? Why is it good news to us? When God bares a holy arm (v. 10), what is being said to those who held Israel captive in Isaiah's time and in Jesus' time? What "principalities and powers" does God's holy arm confront today?

Why do you think Luke 2:1-7 gives so much detail about the political situation? Why do you think the shepherds were the first to hear the news of Jesus' birth? How do the shepherds treat the news? What is unexpected in their behavior?

PRAYER

God of glory, we praise you for the strength of your holy arm, and give thanks that you are not only "with us" but also "for us." We pray for new parents everywhere and ask you to give them Mary's love and Joseph's courage. Help us all watch over the children in our dangerous and troubled world. Give us peace on earth and help us live always in the favor of your grace, for the sake of your Son. Amen.

Day 4

SCRIPTURE

Read Psalm 98 aloud.
Read 2 Samuel 7:1-13 and John 1:1-14.

IMAGES

What do you imagine the Word's role in Creation to be? (See

John 1:1-4.) In Proverbs 8:22-31, the voice of Wisdom playfully suggests that during Creation there was a companion, a skilled worker, someone to delight in newly created humanity, sharing the work with God. Imagine now the delight God shares with Jesus over God's "new creation."

Remember playing with a flashlight as a child, covering it with your hand and seeing the light still shining through? Why does that experience often comfort a child? Why are most children afraid of the dark? How do parents comfort children who are afraid? What happens to our fears when the light of Jesus comes into our lives?

REFLECTIONS

Nathan tells David that the home God prefers is a tent (2 Sam. 7:6-7). Commentaries on John 1:14 point out that the word here translated "lived among us" comes from the same root word as *tent* or *tabernacle* and therefore means literally "pitched a tent among us." What is the significance of God living in a tent?

The people of Israel knew that God's glory filled the Tabernacle, the shepherds saw God's glory shining around them (Luke 2:9), and we see God's glory in Jesus Christ who lives among us. We sometimes sing the old hymn "In the Cross of Christ I Glory." Reflect on what happens when we see God's glory. Light and life are linked in John 1:4. In what ways does the coming of the "true light" (v. 9) give us fullness of life?

PRAYER

God of light and life, we are thankful that you make your home with us and that you make a home for us. Help us see your glory in our homes and in the church that loves and serves you. Lead us to bring the light of your glory to the people who sit in the shadow of death. Make your presence known to us wherever we go and show us how to live always in your light. In the name of your Son. Amen.

Day 5

SCRIPTURE

Read Psalm 98 aloud.
Read John 3:1-17 and Romans 5:8-11.
Read "Hark! the Herald Angels Sing."

IMAGES

"Lifted up" in John 3:14 and John 12:32 is an image that leads to a variety of associations. Focus first on the healing image of the serpent lifted up by Moses, then on Jesus lifted up on the Cross for us and for all people, then on God's lifting up Jesus from the tomb, and finally on Jesus' name lifted up above every name.

Imagine a scene around a Christmas tree with a gathering of friends or family. What brings them together? Are they at peace with each other? Imagine two people who have been in conflict with each other meeting under the branches of a large tree. What can they say or do to heal the hurt and bring about reconciliation? Imagine another tree, the tree of reconciliation with God (Rom. 5:10). What things have separated us from God in the past? How do you picture God bringing us together?

REFLECTIONS

What do the familiar verses in John 3:1-17 add to our understanding of Jesus' coming, and why do they belong with the Christmas story? Reflect on the various meanings of descending and ascending in verses 13-15. Can you name three "descents"—one in the future—and three "ascents" associated with Jesus? Whom does Jesus come to save, according to verse 17?

When we sing "peace on earth and mercy mild," what do we mean by "peace" and "mercy"? In listening to "Hark! the Herald Angels Sing," we may hear "S-u-n of Righteousness" as "S-o-n of Righteousness." What does "righteousness" mean, and how is Jesus both "Sun" and "Son"? What do you understand the gift of "light and life" to be? Is this the same as "eternal life" (John 3:15)? After reading John 3:3-8, reflect on the meaning of the hymn phrase "born to give us second birth." Jesus rises "with healing in his wings." How is Jesus' resurrection a healing event for us?

PRAYER

Holy God, Jesus was born that we no more may die. Give us grace to walk always in the light of Jesus and cast away all our fears. Show us this Christmas the depth of your love, and help us welcome the free gift of your Son who came to save the world. Teach us the angels' song of peace that we may praise your glory and spread to all the world your righteousness and mercy. In Jesus' name. Amen.

Day 6

SCRIPTURE

Read Psalm 98 aloud.
Read Isaiah 9:2-7 and Titus 3:4-7.

IMAGES

Picture again the familiar images from Luke 2:16-19, focusing on the stable, Mary and Joseph, and the baby in the manger. Think of the beginning of Jesus' life in a stable made in a cave; the wrapping of the baby in swaddling clothes by a woman named Mary; and the tender, watchful care of a man named Joseph. Now read Luke 23:50-56 and look for similar images (see Luke 24:10 for the names of the women mentioned here).

What images in Isaiah 9:2-7 reminded the early Christians of the announcement of Jesus' birth and the purpose of his coming? Reflect on the similarities of the images in Isaiah 9:2 and John 1:3-6. Compare the images in Isaiah 9:3-4 and Matthew 11:28-30.

REFLECTIONS

What signs of God's new creation are visible in Isaiah 9:5–7? Look for indications of disarmament; changes in who has power and authority; and the promise of a reign of justice, righteousness, and endless peace.

Make a list of negative attitudes that are sometimes exhibited during the busy time of preparing for Christmas, and think of ways they can be changed using Titus 3:4-7 and Philippians 4:4-7 as a guide.

PRAYER

Loving and kind God, you have saved us according to your mercy. Help us, like the women named Mary and the men named Joseph in the Gospel, care for the very young, for the unjustly condemned, and for the dying. Keep us mindful of the needs of others as we celebrate the coming of your Son that we may rise joyful with all nations and give glory to the newborn King. In Jesus' name. Amen.

Christmas Week

✺

EXPECTING CHRIST'S REIGN TO BEGIN NOW

"Where is the child who has been born king of the Jews?
For we observed his star at its rising,
and have come to pay him homage."

— MATTHEW 2:2

The Christmas story is filled with joy and love: a newborn baby, a sweet young mother, shepherds and sheep, angels singing, and a night filled with stars. The goodness of God's love for the world shines above everything else and lights our Christmas celebrations, making them among our most treasured times together as a community.

However, a background of treachery and greed lies underneath the familiar story, and some of the plot developments are not entirely suitable for young children to hear. We see a proud and pretentious emperor bent on dominating the world, ruthless soldiers occupying a poor country, a puppet king so determined to insure his own succession that he resorts to the massacre of children. Herod's slaughter of the innocents is more than a shocking postscript; it signals the urgency of Christ's coming. It is a sign of the defiance that continues today against God's rule, a rampage of death that spurns God's gift of life. All our attempts to dismiss this part of the story as something that happened only in an ancient, brutal period of history fly in the face of the children we see on the nightly news—dying as innocent casualties of war, ravaged by famine and disease, massacred by terrorists, victimized by domestic quarrels, or killed by classmates whose despair and desperation lead to violence.

The birth story in Matthew tells of several magi, court scholars who studied the stars and reported their findings to their king. They traveled from a far country, probably Persia, seeking a new king, and their reasons for such an undertaking are unclear. Perhaps they had heard ancient stories told in Persia of prophecies learned from the Hebrew exiles about a king who would one day come to rule the world in mercy and peace. Perhaps the light they had seen in the night sky held a message so compelling that they couldn't resist. Perhaps they were simply tired of court intrigues and an inept ruling party and went in search of something better. Whatever their reasons, we think of them as seekers after a new rule for life, and their journey has inspired seekers ever since. They were willing to leave home, endure hardship, and persist across desert and mountain with no clear destination, all for what must have seemed to their colleagues back home a foolish dream.

The magi probably carried with them letters of introduction from their king, so the obvious thing to do was pay a courtesy call on King Herod and see what information he had. They didn't get to see Herod at first, of course, but they asked his minions the crucial question, one that would set off a series of tragic events and alert the forces that would seek

Jesus' death, and lead to his crucifixion as "King of the Jews" more than thirty years later. In all innocence they asked, "Where is the child who has been born king of the Jews?" (Matt. 2:2). As soon as he heard, Herod called them in secretly and in his best ingratiating manner asked to be kept up to speed on their findings. He could not stand the thought of another king. In the end neither could Rome or the religious authorities who had made a convenient accommodation with Rome.

Herod's reaction to the news of Jesus' birth is the first clue that, though he came with no weapons and no army, everything Jesus did was an affront to the empire. There was no room for Jesus in Caesar's plans for the world. Jesus came to begin a reign that would in every way be distinguished from his. Augustus Caesar claimed a miraculous birth and the right to be worshiped as a divinity. But Jesus was truly God's only begotten Son. The cry of Jesus' followers after the Resurrection became, "Jesus Christ is Lord," and it was their way of defying Caesar, of saying, "Caesar is not our lord."

Rome's power lay in its great army and innovative military tactics; Jesus' power evidences itself in his suffering love and comes from the God of life who raised Jesus from the dead. Jesus stands in contrast today to would-be emperors, those who put the lives and livelihood of others in jeopardy to further their own political or corporate greed. Rome restricted citizenship to a few—privileged by birth or rich enough to buy it—but Jesus opened citizenship in his reign to all who came to him. Jesus' reign has no problem with illegal aliens because all are welcomed as citizens and heirs. "So then you are no longer strangers and aliens, but you are citizens with the saints and also members of the household of God, built upon the foundation of the apostles and prophets, with Christ Jesus himself as the cornerstone" (Eph. 2:19-20).

Those of us who live in a modern democratic state sometimes hesitate to use the word *king* in reference to Jesus. For us the term seems obsolete, a remnant of a bygone patriarchal monarchy. In the United States we had enough of kings with George III, thank you; furthermore, we don't like kings because monarchies favor men over women and royalty over ordinary citizens and usually result in exploitation. But *king* is a term that carries deep mythical and psychological connotations that are still in our consciousness; it represents a reality about people and power we can't deny. Children still wear crowns at birthday parties, Cinderella is still a favorite story, and pretending to be a royal court is still a part of children's play. As older children, we "kinged" our checkers, checkmated kings in chess, and probably played some version of "king of the hill." In college we may have studied Shakespeare's intriguing but flawed kings in the history plays and in *King Lear.*

King, like any effective metaphor, has painful edges, and the pain is part of the reason the word still resonates. We may not have experienced a king who is head of state, but we have a good idea of the negative aspects of being ruled by a king. We have all known people who acted as if they were king or queen with the right to decide everything for us—possibly an overbearing parent or spouse, a boss, a CEO bent on personal gain, a government leader whose head was turned by power. And we all know of tyrants and oppressive regimes the world over that deny the fullness of life to the people. Jesus came as king to confront such arrogance, to "[scatter] the proud in the thoughts of their hearts" (Luke 1:51).

If Jesus Christ rules in our lives, then no one can "lord it over us." Jesus brings with him a reversal of the usual idea of kingship, a new reality that opposes tyrants and ushers in a reign of mercy and peace, mutuality and harmony. Jesus called himself servant and shepherd; others gave him the title king, sometimes in mockery rather than in honor. African American slaves recognized this new kind of king in Jesus and sang about it with great hope in spirituals: "King Jesus rides on a milk-white horse"; "King Jesus is a-listening all day long." What other king has ever been known as the One who listens when we cry out to him? King Jesus is the hope of oppressed people from the 1920s Mexican resistance movement whose rallying cry was *Viva Cristo Rey!* ("Long live Christ the King!") to artists who for generations have pictured Christ the Victor ruling all creation after he has scattered the tyrants and put all enemies under his footstool. What other king would come as a household slave and suffer a humiliating, painful death on a cross for us?

Jesus preached that the kingdom is already at hand, to be enjoyed now in the company of other disciples. We as Christians are to bring others—the weak, the abandoned, the needy, the lost—into it.

Christmas celebrates the birth of our Savior and Lord, but sometimes we act as if we think salvation is only about securing a place for ourselves as individuals in Christ's heavenly kingdom, like James and John who asked Jesus for a seat of honor (Mark 10:35-37). Jesus, however, preached that the kingdom is already at hand, to be enjoyed now in the company of other disciples, and we as Christians are to bring others—the weak, the abandoned, the needy, the lost—into it. Jesus came to save the whole world (John 3:16-17), and we, as stewards of Christ's reign now, are called to work for the fullness of life—including life's essentials of food, shelter, clothing, health care, education, security—to all earth's inhabitants. Like the just ruler described in Psalm 72, we are called to "defend the cause of the poor of the people, give deliverance to the needy, and crush the oppressor" (v. 4).

The "world" that Jesus came to save is represented in the birth stories by two groups of people who could hardly be more varied: shepherds from the nearby hillsides and wealthy sages from a foreign land. Farmworkers and well-connected intellectuals, one group from the neighborhood and one who traveled from a far country. No one is a foreigner at the manger; no one is excluded because of economic class. God wants a full table at the heavenly banquet and is willing to look for dinner guests in unexpected places. Our place in Christ's reign means that we are willing to sit next to someone who appears at first to be alien to us but turns out to be a citizen, a member with us of God's own household. Embraced by this communion of love, we realize our call to the life of the Spirit and enjoy the fullness of life that comes with Christ's reign of justice and peace.

HYMN FOR THE WEEK

"Rejoice, the Lord Is King" (*UMH* #715, *NCH* #303, *EH* #481, *PH* #155, *LBW* #171, *AMECH* #89, *TBH* #197)

Rejoice, the Lord is King! Your Lord and King adore;
mortals, give thanks and sing, and triumph evermore.
Lift up your heart, lift up your voice;
rejoice; again I say, rejoice.

Jesus the Savior reigns, the God of truth and love;
when he had purged our stains, he took his seat above.
Lift up your heart, lift up your voice;
rejoice; again I say, rejoice.

[God's] kingdom cannot fail;
Christ rules o'er earth and heaven;
the keys of earth and hell are to our Jesus given.
Lift up your heart, lift up your voice;
rejoice; again I say, rejoice.
Rejoice in glorious hope! Jesus the Judge shall come,
and take his servants up to their eternal home.
We soon shall hear th' archangel's voice;
the trump of God shall sound, rejoice!

—CHARLES WESLEY, 1746

"Rejoice, the Lord Is King" gives us reason to praise Jesus as the just ruler God has promised, recalling the events we celebrate at Epiphany and the story of Jesus' kingship throughout the Gospels. The genealogy in Matthew 1:1-17 traces Jesus' ancestry to the royal line of David. In chapter 2, the magi's search for the child who has been born king of the Jews reveals Jesus' identity as the One anointed to bring God's reign. The nature of the reign Jesus came to begin is apparent both in the violent reaction of Herod and the worshipful joy of the magi. We learn more about Jesus' reign in the kingdom parables and through Jesus' all-encompassing love and ministry to the outcasts. Jesus further incites his enemies by his ride into Jerusalem on a donkey, the obligatory steed of ancient Hebrew kings returning from a victory (Zech. 9:9), and then is crucified under the inscription "King of the Jews."

If the bringing of Jesus' reign began with pain and reactionary violence, why then are we to rejoice? The second stanza points to the victory: Jesus, the God of truth and love, endured suffering to free us from the tyranny of sin and death. Following his great act of love, he takes "his seat above"; that is, he is exalted and given the "name that is above every name, so that at the name of Jesus every knee should bend, in heaven and on earth and under the earth, and every tongue should confess that Jesus Christ is Lord" (Phil. 2:9-11). In the third stanza, Jesus is given the keys to both earth and hell (see Rev. 1:18). Jesus Christ, in other words, will redeem all creation.

The final stanza reminds us that our hope for the future lies in God's promise to bring us into our eternal home, where Christ reigns with God and the Holy Spirit, where we are embraced by the love and joy of God and the communion of saints. The fulfillment of Jesus' reign will come when God's trumpet sounds and "we will be changed" (1 Cor. 15:52).

DAILY SCRIPTURE READINGS

Isaiah 60:1-6; Matthew 2:1-18; John 18:33-38; 19:16-22; 20:15-18; Psalm 72; Ephesians 2:17-22; Matthew 25:31-40; John 21:15-19; Ephesians 3:7-21; Colossians 3:12-17; Revelation 7:9-17

PSALM FOR THE WEEK

Read Psalm 148 aloud every day.

Day 1

SCRIPTURE

Read aloud Psalm 148.
Read Isaiah 60:1-6 and Matthew 2:1-18.

IMAGES

Isaiah 60:1-6 pictures a joyous homecoming celebration. What details in these verses remind us of the story of the visit of the magi? How do the images reflect the theme of epiphany or the revelation of God? What do you remember about the wise men from Epiphany celebrations or pageants? In what ways are the remembered images different from what we know about the travelers in Matthew's story? What costumes other than royal robes would be appropriate for the magi? What would be an effective way to show that they are foreigners?

REFLECTIONS

Reflect on the giving of gifts in today's readings: the restoration of sons and daughters, flocks, and prosperity in Isaiah; the gift of praise; the significance of the magi's gifts in Matthew; God's gift to us of the Light of the world.

Whom do you think the magi expected to find at the end of their journey? What do you think caused them to be "overwhelmed with joy" (v. 10)? What happens in Matthew 2:1-18 that warns readers of Jesus' trial and crucifixion?

PRAYER

God of light, you sent the star to show the magi the way. Guide us when we seek your truth. When shadows cover the earth, help us wait for your glory to rise upon us. When children are endangered by troubles of any kind, show us the way to comfort and protect them. Give us courage always to arise and let our light shine for your glory. In the name of Jesus. Amen.

Day 2

SCRIPTURE

Read aloud Psalm 148.

Read John 18:33-38; 19:16-22; 20:15-18.

IMAGES

Imagine the puzzlement of those who read the inscription on the cross of Jesus. Crucifixion was the punishment for insurrectionists and runaway slaves. Does Jesus have anything in common with either of these? How could a king be crucified? Imagine the garden where Mary Magdalene, mistaking Jesus for the gardener, asks where Jesus' body has been moved. Think of her reaction when she recognizes Jesus. Imagine Jesus' voice when he calls her name. Imagine Jesus calling your name.

REFLECTIONS

In John 18:33-38, what does Jesus tell Pilate about the origins of his kingdom? What about Jesus' response in verse 37 reminds you of the good shepherd of John 10:3-4? What do we know about truth if we live in Jesus' kingdom?

In what way was the inscription on the cross both an indictment of Jesus under Roman law and a statement about Jesus' identity (John 19:21-22)? Look at what Jesus says to Mary Magdalene in John 20:17. Why is it urgent that Jesus return to reign at the right hand of God? (See also Phil. 2:9-11.) What mission does he give her?

PRAYER

Jesus, you are the Ruler of all earth and heaven. Listen to us in our despair over the troubles around us. Teach us to know you as the truth, that we may find in you the way to life. Be present with those who are condemned for standing up against the enemies of your rule of love and life. Give us courage to embrace all people in your name. Amen.

Day 3

SCRIPTURE

Read aloud Psalm 148.
Read Psalm 72 and Ephesians 2:17-22.

IMAGES

Reflect on each of these images in Psalm 72: a just ruler reigns faithfully like the sun and moon; he or she is like showers that water the earth; kings and nations pay homage to the ruler and wish him or her happiness; an abundance of grain waves from the mountaintops; God, whose glory fills the earth, is praised. Read "Hail to the Lord's Anointed," a hymn based on this psalm.[3]

Hail to the Lord's Anointed, great David's greater Son!
Hail in the time appointed, his reign on earth begun!
He comes to break oppression, to set the captive free;
to take away transgression, and rule in equity.

He comes with succor speedy to those who suffer wrong;
to help the poor and needy, and bid the weak be strong;

to give them songs for sighing, their darkness turn to light,
whose souls, condemned and dying, are precious in his sight.

He shall come down like showers upon the fruitful earth;
love, joy, and hope, like flowers, spring in his path to birth.
Before him, on the mountains, shall peace, the herald go,
and righteousness, in fountains, from hill to valley flow.

To him shall prayer unceasing and daily vows ascend;
his kingdom still increasing, a kingdom without end.
The tide of time shall never his covenant remove;
his name shall stand forever; that name to us is love.

—JAMES MONTGOMERY, 1821

How do you imagine Jesus proclaiming peace far and near (Eph. 2:17)? What images come to your mind when you think of the phrases "no longer strangers" and "members of the household of God" (v. 19)?

REFLECTIONS

Psalm 72, traditionally thought to be a prayer of David for the future King Solomon, describes the attributes of a just ruler. What qualities and policies does the psalm advocate? Is it possible to apply these same qualifications to elected officials today? Why do you think the early church used this psalm to praise Jesus for his reign? Why is this psalm often read on Epiphany?

What responsibilities and privileges come from being a citizen of Christ's reign (Eph. 2:19)? What do we learn about the foundation of our faith from verse 20? What do verses 21-22 say about the place of the community in our faith?

PRAYER

God of glory, you alone have done wondrous things. We thank you that you have made us members of your household. Build us together spiritually and make us worthy to be your dwelling place. Send us in your name to proclaim peace and to deliver the poor and those who have no helper. For Jesus' sake. Amen.

Day 4

SCRIPTURE

Read aloud Psalm 148.
Read Matthew 25:31-40 and John 21:15-19.

IMAGES

How do you picture Jesus coming as a judge? Do we need to be fearful of Jesus? Why or why not? Picture in your mind outreach programs in your congregation that serve needs in the ways described in Matthew 25:35-40. How do you relate to people you see as needy?

Picture the scene on the beach after Jesus has cooked breakfast for the disciples (see John 21:15-19). The good smells of a hot meal still linger. The lake shimmers in the morning sun. The peace of Jesus' presence and the joy of his resurrection live in the hearts of Jesus' friends. Why is Peter uncomfortable? How does Jesus help him see his place in Jesus' reign?

Look back at Mary's song (Luke 1:46-55) and Jesus' preaching (Luke 4:16-21). How does Matthew 25:31-40 relate to these readings? What accountability to Jesus do we have as members of God's household? Do we help people in order to be saved or because that is who we are as members of Jesus' family?

John's Gospel proclaims a God of love; Jesus' coming forms a community of love. What does John 21:15-19 say about love and our responsibility to one another? What do you think Jesus meant for Peter to do when he told him to feed and tend the sheep and lambs?

PRAYER

Jesus, our Lord and our friend, feed us as you fed the disciples on the beach. Fill our hunger with your love, and guide us with your Spirit to see the needs of those around us. Help us live in such a way that the forgotten and abandoned members of your family have all they need for life. Bring us into communion around your table with all our sisters and brothers. Amen.

Day 5

SCRIPTURE

Read aloud Psalm 148.
Read Ephesians 3:7-21 and Colossians 3:12-17.

IMAGES

When we sing "Come, Thou Long-Expected Jesus," we pray for Jesus to deliver the people and set them free. We also pray for Jesus to "rule in all our hearts alone." Think of an image or an icon that speaks to you of Jesus ruling in your heart. It can be a Christian symbol, a picture you remember, or something from your own imagination. How does the way we live change under Jesus' rule?

Think of an image that speaks to you of what it is like to be clothed with love (Col. 3:14).

REFLECTIONS

According to Colossians 3:12-13, what are the characteristics of members of God's household? What activities does Colossians 3:16-17 suggest to show that the peace of Christ rules in your heart?

Reflect on each of the following phrases from Ephesians 3:7-21: "boundless riches of Christ," "the wisdom of God in its rich variety," "in accordance with the eternal purpose that [God] has carried out in Christ Jesus our Lord," "from whom every family in heaven and on earth takes its name," "Christ may dwell in your hearts through faith," "rooted and grounded in love," and "to know the love of Christ that surpasses knowledge." What do these verses say about Christ's reign now?

PRAYER

God of all the earth, you are able to accomplish abundantly far more than we can ask or imagine. Fill us with your fullness. Teach us the breadth and length and height and depth of your love. Gather us into the community of your saints, ready to receive Jesus and bring his healing and peace to the world. In Jesus' name we pray. Amen.

Day 6

Read aloud Psalm 148.
Read Revelation 7:9-17.
Read "Rejoice, the Lord Is King."

IMAGES

What pictures do you remember from a church, museum, or book of religious art that show Jesus as the Lamb of God? What do they show about Jesus' suffering love? Can you think of one that shows Jesus on the throne of God or ruling with God? Read the hymn "What Wondrous Love Is This."[4]

> What wondrous love is this, O my soul, O my soul,
> what wondrous love is this, O my soul!
> What wondrous love is that that caused the Lord of bliss
> to bear the dreadful curse for my soul, for my soul,
> to bear the dreadful curse for my soul.
>
> What wondrous love is this, O my soul, O my soul,
> what wondrous love is this, O my soul!
> What wondrous love is this, that caused the Lord of life,
> to lay aside his crown for my soul, for my soul,
> to lay aside his crown for my soul.
>
> To God and to the Lamb I will sing, I will sing,
> to God and to the Lamb, I will sing;

to God and to the Lamb who is the great I AM,
while millions join the theme I will sing, I will sing,
while millions join the theme I will sing.

—USA FOLK HYMN

Sometimes we see cartoons of people in heaven sitting on clouds looking bored. How is the picture of God's redeemed people in Revelation 7:9-17 different from that image? The Greek word for "worship" in verse 15 can also be translated "work"; the New English Bible translates this phrase as "minister to him day and night." What activity does this suggest? Look also at the last stanza of "Love Divine, All Loves Excelling" (p. 47).

REFLECTIONS

John the Baptist calls Jesus the "Lamb of God who takes away the sin of the world" in John 1:29. What events bring the Lamb from his baptism by John to the "center of the throne" (Rev. 7:17)? What does verse 9 tell us about the people who are gathered before the Lamb? How can Jesus be both shepherd (v. 17) and Lamb? How will the Lamb care for the redeemed (vv. 16-17)?

Look at John 1:29, Philippians 2:7-9, and stanza 2 of "Rejoice, the Lord Is King" (p. 80); then look at Revelation 1:18 and stanza 3; and finally look at 1 Corinthians 15:51-52 and stanza 4. Reflect on the biblical sources of Wesley's hymn. What reasons does this hymn give for us to rejoice?

PRAYER

Jesus our shepherd, you are the Lamb of God who has come to free us and heal us. Give us courage to rejoice in your

name and bring your hope to our world of trouble and conflict. Give us grace to look for your coming in glory and to
join the saints gathered before your throne, singing and blessing you day and night, in praise and thanksgiving for your
wondrous love. Amen.

Leader's Guide

FOR SMALL-GROUP DISCUSSIONS

✿

Week 1

PREPARING

Prepare the room by arranging chairs in a circle and covering a table (worship center) with a purple or blue cloth. Place a cross at the center of the table. Put four pillar candles on the table and surround them with evergreens. This week light only one candle. Have the words to the hymn and the psalm available for everyone. Find a print or a Christmas card with a depiction of the "peaceable kingdom" (Isa. 11:1-10) to tape to the wall or display on an easel. The American artist Edward Hicks (1780–1849) has more than a hundred paintings on this theme; information is available on the Internet.

Opening Prayer

Ask someone ahead of time to lead the opening prayer. Have index cards available for participants to list prayer concerns as they enter the room and give them to the prayer leader.

Scripture Reading

Take turns reading aloud the following verses.

In days to come
the mountain of the LORD's house
shall be established as the highest of the mountains,
and shall be raised above the hills;
all the nations shall stream to it.
Many peoples shall come and say,
"Come, let us go up to the mountain of the LORD,
to the house of the God of Jacob;
that [God] may teach us [God']s ways
and that we may walk in [God's] paths." (Isa. 2:2-3)

The wolf shall live with the lamb,
the leopard shall lie down with the kid,
the calf and the lion and the fatling together,
and a little child shall lead them.
. . . .
They will not hurt or destroy
on all my holy mountain;
for the earth will be full of the knowledge of the LORD
as the waters cover the sea. (Isa. 11:6, 9)
O that you would tear open the heavens and come down,
so that the mountains would quake at your presence.
. . . .
Yet, O LORD, you are our Father;

we are the clay, and you are our potter;
we are all the work of your hand. (Isa. 64:1, 8)

Therefore we have been buried with him by baptism into death, so that, just as Christ was raised from the dead by the glory of the Father, so we too might walk in newness of life. (Rom. 6:4)

Besides this, you know what time it is, how it is now the moment for you to wake from sleep. For salvation is nearer to us now than when we became believers. (Rom. 13:11)

I am confident of this, that the one who began a good work among you will bring it to completion by the day of Jesus Christ. (Phil. 1:6)

So if anyone is in Christ, there is a new creation: everything old has passed away; see, everything has become new! All this is from God, who reconciled us to himself through Christ, and has given us the ministry of reconciliation. (2 Cor. 5:17-18)

"Then they will see 'the Son of Man coming in a cloud' with power and great glory. Now when these things begin to take place, stand up and raise your heads, because your redemption is drawing near." (Luke 21:27-28)

Look! He is coming with the clouds;
every eye will see him,
even those who pierced him;
and on his account all the tribes of the earth will wail.
So it is to be. Amen.
"I am the Alpha and the Omega," says the Lord God,
who is and who was and who is to come,
the Almighty. (Rev. 1:7-8)

Then I saw a new heaven and a new earth; for the first heaven and the first earth had passed away, and the sea was no more. Then he said to me, "It is done! I am the Alpha and the Omega, the beginning and the end. To the thirsty I will give water as a gift from the spring of the water of life. Those who conquer will inherit these things, and I will be their God and they will be my children." (Rev. 21:1, 6-7)

RESPONSIVE READING

Read Psalm 25:1-10, alternating verses between the leader and group.

SHARING QUESTIONS AND INSIGHTS

Allow time for participants to ask questions or share thoughts that arose during their reading.

HYMN

Read or sing "Lo, He Comes with Clouds Descending" (p. 18). Look carefully at the words. Describe the subject of each stanza. What do you find surprising or puzzling about the hymn's message?

REFLECTION QUESTIONS

How does the hymn help us prepare to celebrate Advent and Christmas? What does it tell us about Jesus' life, death, resurrection, ascension, and second Advent?

What does the hymn say to us about God's new creation? How do you respond to being called a "new creation" in Christ (2 Cor. 5:17)? What is your responsibility as Christ's new creation? What part does the community of faith play in your life as a "new creation"?

What is "new" about Jesus' coming in the birth stories of Luke and Matthew, in our lives today, and "with the clouds" at the end times? What are some of the ways we can see already that God is making "all things new"?

How can we be at home with God?

TELLING THE STORY

Ask the group to put today's discussion in narrative form, so that it becomes a part of the whole story of the coming of Jesus Christ. Begin with this idea in mind: telling a good story sometimes means starting at the end and working backward. The story we tell at Christmas of Jesus' birth is not yet complete, but we know how it will end because we have observed God's "awesome deeds" and we believe God's promise that Jesus will come again in clouds of glory. Include in your narrative visions of God's reign at the end times from the Hebrew prophets, the Gospels, and Revelation. Use as part of the story the events and ideas alluded to in the hymn. End with this affirmation: "Christ has come; Christ is with us; Christ will come again."

CLOSING PRAYER

"Everlasting God, come down!" Keep us awake and ready to receive you. Teach us to prepare for your coming reign and to live now with love, mercy, and kindness toward all the earth. Help us recognize Jesus when he comes and see him now in the faces of loved ones, of strangers, and of those in need. Hold in your arms all those who are sick or sorrowing, and give us your peace. In Jesus' name. Amen.

Leader: The peace of Christ go with you.
Group: **And also with you. Amen.**

Week 2

PREPARING

For a visual focus this session, ask participants ahead of time to bring depictions of some of the images in the readings—a highway, a prisoner being freed, a shepherd, an art print of John the Baptist, a photo of a mountain stream, for example—and tape them to the board or easel. Prepare the room and worship center as you did last week. Light two candles on the Advent Wreath. Have the words to the hymn and the psalm available for everyone.

OPENING PRAYER

Ask someone ahead of time to lead the opening prayer. Have index cards available for participants to list prayer concerns as they enter the room and give them to the prayer leader.

SCRIPTURE READING

Take turns reading aloud the following verses.

> Then the eyes of the blind shall be opened,
>   and the ears of the deaf unstopped;
> then the lame shall leap like a deer,

and the tongue of the speechless sing for joy.
For waters shall break forth in the wilderness
and streams in the desert. (Isa. 35:5-6)

See, the Lord GOD comes with might,
and his arm rules for him;
his reward is with him,
and his recompense before him.
He will feed his flock like a shepherd;
he will gather the lambs in his arms,
and carry them in his bosom,
and gently lead the mother sheep. (Isa. 40:10-11)

The angel said to him, "Do not be afraid, Zechariah, for your prayer has been heard. Your wife Elizabeth will bear you a son, and you will name him John. You will have joy and gladness, and many will rejoice at his birth, for he will be great in the sight of the Lord." (Luke 1:13-15)

As the people were filled with expectation, and all were questioning in their hearts concerning John, whether he might be the Messiah, John answered all of them by saying, "I baptize you with water; but one who is more powerful than I is coming: I am not worthy to untie the thong of his sandals. He will baptize you with the Holy Spirit and fire." (Luke 3:15-16)

For I the LORD love justice,
I hate robbery and wrongdoing;
I will faithfully give them their recompense,
and I will make an everlasting covenant with them.
. . . .
For as the earth brings forth its shoots
and as a garden causes what is sown in it to spring up,

so the Lord GOD will cause righteousness and praise
to spring up before all the nations. (Isa. 61:8, 11)

[Jesus] unrolled the scroll and found the place where it
was written:
"The Spirit of the Lord is upon me,
because he has anointed me
to bring good news to the poor.
He has sent me to proclaim release to the captives
and recovery of sight to the blind,
to let the oppressed go free,
to proclaim the year of the Lord's favor." (Luke 4:17-19)

When John heard in prison what the Messiah was doing, he sent
word by his disciples and said to him, "Are you the one who is to
come, or are we to wait for another?" Jesus answered them, "Go and
tell John what you hear and see: the blind receive their sight, the lame
walk, the lepers are cleansed, the deaf hear, the dead are raised, and
the poor have good news brought to them." (Matt. 11:2-5)

When the fullness of time had come, God sent his Son, born of a
woman, born under the law, in order to redeem those who were
under the law, so that we might receive adoption as children. . . .
So you are no longer a slave but a child, and if a child then also an
heir, through God. (Gal. 4:4-5, 7)

Let the same mind be in you that was in Christ Jesus,
who, though he was in the form of God,
did not regard equality with God
as something to be exploited,
but emptied himself,
taking the form of a slave,
being born in human likeness. (Phil. 2:5-7)

The Spirit and the bride say, "Come."
And let everyone who hears say, "Come."
And let everyone who is thirsty come.
Let anyone who wishes take the water of life as a gift. . . .
The one who testifies to these things says, "Surely I am
coming soon."
Amen. Come, Lord Jesus! (Rev. 22:17, 20)

RESPONSIVE READING

Read responsively Psalm 85 or Isaiah 40:1-11. Listen to the words of Isaiah 40:1-7 as they are sung on a recording of Handel's *Messiah*. A good recent recording is by the King's College Choir from the Decca Record Company Limited, 1994, London.

SHARING QUESTIONS AND INSIGHTS

Allow time for participants to ask questions or share thoughts that arose during their reading.

HYMN

Read or sing "Come, Thou Long-Expected Jesus." Look carefully at the words to the hymn. Describe the subject of each stanza. What do you find surprising or puzzling about the hymn's message?

REFLECTION QUESTIONS

Reflect on what we learn about God's relationship with the people from the images in Isaiah 40:1-11; for example: "wilderness," "highway," "valleys lifted up," and "the grass withers." What is meant by "God's glory" in Isaiah 40:5 and by "Glory to God in the highest" in the angels' song (Luke 2:14)? Talk about the images in Isaiah 40:10-11: God comes in might and rules with a strong arm (v. 10); God comes tenderly leading and feeding the sheep, carrying the lambs (v. 11).

Why is Zechariah afraid in Luke 1:12? Have you experienced an answer to prayer that was unexpected and in some way frightening? Why were some people frightened by John's coming and by Jesus' coming?

Isaiah 61:8 declares that God is a lover of justice. What does justice have to do with repentance? (See Luke 3:10-14.) How is God's love of justice shown in Jesus' sermon in Luke 4:14-24?

Ask someone to give background on the hymn Paul uses in Philippians 2:5-11 and its importance in the tradition of the church. In the scripture index of the hymnal, find hymns based on this text and read them. What do these verses tell us about who Jesus is? How can you use these concepts to talk about what we mean by the Incarnation? What themes in these verses are echoed in "Come, Thou Long-Expected Jesus"?

TELLING THE STORY

Ask the group to put today's discussion in narrative form, so that it becomes part of the whole story of the coming of Jesus Christ. Begin with these ideas: The story of John the Baptist introduces the story of Jesus' coming, now and at the end times. John's story echoes the miraculous birth stories of the Hebrew Bible and foreshadows Jesus' birth, life, and death. The preaching of both John and Jesus was in the tradition of the Hebrew prophets, and both proclaimed God's reign to be near. Note similarities in their words and Isaiah's words. John also points to the ways Jesus is greater than he. Use as part of the story the events and ideas alluded to in the hymn.

End with this affirmation: "Christ has come; Christ is with us; Christ will come again."

CLOSING PRAYER

God, we know you love justice. Teach us your ways of compassion for all people. Help us live so that everyone enjoys the bountiful gifts you so graciously give to the earth. Restore us to the life of community and well-being that your mercy and steadfast love make possible. Come to us now in the midst of sorrow and trouble; scatter the clouds of doubt, and free us from our fears. Come, Lord Jesus!

> Leader: The peace of Christ go with you.
> Group: **And also with you. Amen.**

Week 3

PREPARING

Prepare the room with chairs in a circle and a table for a worship center covered in purple or blue cloth. Place a cross at the center of the table. Place four pillar candles on the table with evergreens around them. Light three candles this week. Have the words to the hymn and the psalm available for everyone. Find one or more representations of the Annunciation—the painting by African American artist Henry Ossawa Tanner, now in the Philadelphia Museum of Art, is one example—to tape to the board or easel.

OPENING PRAYER

Ask someone ahead of time to lead the opening prayer. Have index cards available for participants to list prayer concerns as they enter the room and give them to the prayer leader.

SCRIPTURE READING

Take turns reading aloud the following verses.

[Jesus] is the image of the invisible God, the firstborn of all creation; for in him all things in heaven and on earth were created, things visible and invisible, . . . —all things have been created through him and for him. He himself is before all things, and in him all things hold together. He is the head of the body, the church; he is the beginning, the firstborn from the dead, so that he might come to have first place in everything. For in him all the fullness of God was pleased to dwell. (Col. 1:15-19)

Therefore the Lord himself will give you a sign. Look, the young woman is with child and shall bear a son, and shall name him Immanuel. (Isa. 7:14)

Now the birth of Jesus the Messiah took place in this way. When his mother Mary had been engaged to Joseph, but before they lived together she was found to be with child from the Holy Spirit. (Matt. 1:18)

When Joseph awoke from sleep, he did as the angel of the Lord commanded him; he took her as his wife, but had no marital relations with her until she had borne a son, and he named him Jesus. (Matt. 1:24-25)

The angel said to her, "Do not be afraid, Mary, for you have found favor with God. And now, you will conceive in your womb and bear a son, and you will name him Jesus. . . . Mary said to the angel, "How can this be, since I am a virgin?" The angel said to her, "The Holy Spirit will come upon you, and the power of the Most High will overshadow you; therefore the child to be born will be holy; he will be called Son of God." (Luke 1:30-31, 34-35)

And Elizabeth was filled with the Holy Spirit and exclaimed with a loud cry, "Blessed are you among women, and blessed is the fruit of your womb. And why has this happened to me, that the mother of my Lord comes to me?" (Luke 1:41-43)

And he shall stand and feed his flock
in the strength of the LORD,
in the majesty of the name of the LORD his God.
And they shall live secure, for now he shall be great
to the ends of the earth;
and he shall be the one of peace. (Mic. 5:4-5)
"Blessed be the Lord God of Israel,
[who] has looked favorably on [the] people and
redeemed them.
[God] has raised up a mighty savior for us
in the house of [God's] servant David." (Luke 1:68-69)

I dwell in the high and holy place,
and also with those who are contrite and humble in spirit,
to revive the spirit of the humble,
and to revive the heart of the contrite.
. . . .
I have seen their ways, but I will heal them;
I will lead them and repay them with comfort,
creating for their mourners the fruit of the lips.

Peace, peace, to the far and the near, says the LORD;
and I will heal them. (Isa. 57:15, 18-19)

May the God of peace . . . sanctify you entirely; and may your spirit and soul and body be kept sound and blameless at the coming of our Lord Jesus Christ. The one who calls you is faithful, and . . . will do this. (1 Thess. 5:23-24)

"Master, now you are dismissing your servant in peace,
according to your word;
for my eyes have seen your salvation,
which you have prepared in the presence of all peoples,
a light for revelation to the Gentiles
and for glory to your people Israel." (Luke 2:29-32)

Paul, a servant of Jesus Christ, called to be an apostle, set apart for the gospel of God, which he promised beforehand through his prophets in the holy scriptures, the gospel concerning his Son, who was descended from David according to the flesh and was declared to be Son of God with power according to the spirit of holiness by resurrection from the dead, Jesus Christ our Lord. (Rom. 1:1-4)

RESPONSIVE READING

Read Mary's Song, Luke 1:46-55 (see p. 46). Or sing this passage as a hymn; see, for example, "My Soul Gives Glory to My God," *UMH* #198, *NCH* #119, *PH* #600.

SHARING QUESTIONS AND INSIGHTS

Allow time for participants to ask questions or share thoughts that arose during their reading.

HYMN

Read or sing "Love Divine, All Loves Excelling." Look carefully at the words to the hymn. Describe the subject of each stanza. What do you find surprising or puzzling about the hymn's message?

REFLECTION QUESTIONS

Look at the three readings for the week from the prophets—Isaiah 7:10-16; Micah 5:2-5; Isaiah 57:14-19—and the hymn "Love Divine, All Loves Excelling." What do they tell us about the God of Israel? How do the images of God in these readings tell us more about who Jesus is and what his coming means?

We sometimes think of the Holy Spirit's arrival only in connection with Pentecost, but the Spirit is found at work already in the first chapters of the Gospels. Look at Matthew 1:18, 20 and Luke 1:35, 41, 67. What is the Spirit's work with Mary, with Elizabeth, and with Zechariah? Reflect on the ways the Spirit helps us know Jesus' presence in our lives and leads us to tell others about Jesus. How is the Spirit depicted in paintings of the Annunciation?

Peace appears frequently in our readings—in Isaiah 57:19; Micah 5:5; Luke 1:79; 1 Thessalonians 5:13, 23; for example—and will come again in the angels' announcement to the shepherds. Why do you think peace is associated with God's salvation? Why does the way of peace sometimes provoke hostility (Luke 12:51)? Why do we greet each other in worship with "the peace of Christ"?

What are the ways the Bible tells us about Jesus' divinity, in addition to the story of his miraculous birth? Describe as many ways as you can think of that Jesus is said to be God's Son in both the Gospels and the Epistles. Talk about the ways the Gospels and Epistles emphasize Jesus' humanity. (See especially Col. 1:15-19 and Rom. 1:1-4.)

TELLING THE STORY

Ask the group to put today's discussion in narrative form, so that it becomes a part of the whole story of the coming of Jesus Christ. Begin with these ideas: The circumstances of Jesus' birth are becoming clearer as we continue the readings. We know now something about Mary and Joseph and the angel's announcement to them. We know about John the Baptist's role. We know the connection of Jesus to his Hebrew ancestors who were expecting God to send a deliverer. We know that Jesus will be born in Bethlehem and will be God's Son as well as Mary's Son. Use as part of the story the events and ideas alluded to in the hymn. End with this affirmation: "Christ has come; Christ is with us; Christ will come again."

CLOSING PRAYER

By your tender mercy, O God, our God,
open our eyes to the dawn breaking on us from on high.
Lead us to bring your light to those who sit in darkness
and in the shadow of death.
Guide our feet into the way of peace.
We ask these things for the sake of Jesus' pure,
unbounded love,
for Jesus Christ, heaven's joy and our compassion. Amen.
—based on Luke 1:78-79

Leader: The peace of Christ go with you.
Group: **And also with you. Amen.**

Week 4

PREPARING

Prepare the room and worship center as in previous weeks. This week light all four candles. Have the words to the hymn and the psalm available for everyone. Find one or more artistic representations of the angels announcing Jesus' birth to the shepherds—from art prints or Christmas cards—to tape to the board or easel.

OPENING PRAYER

Ask someone ahead of time to lead the opening prayer. Have index cards available for participants to list prayer concerns as they enter the room and give them to the prayer leader.

SCRIPTURE READING

Take turns reading aloud the following verses:

> Do not fear, for I have redeemed you;
> I have called you by name, you are mine.
> When you pass through the waters, I will be with you;
> and through the rivers, they shall not overwhelm you;
> when you walk through fire you shall not be burned,
> and the flame shall not consume you.
> For I am the LORD your God,
> the Holy One of Israel, your Savior. (Isa. 43:1*b*-3)

Let your gentleness be known to everyone. The Lord is near. Do not worry about anything, but in everything by prayer and supplication with thanksgiving let your requests be made known to God. And the peace of God, which surpasses all understanding, will guard your hearts and your minds in Christ Jesus. (Phil. 4:5-7)

"I am the God of your father, the God of Abraham, the God of Isaac, and the God of Jacob. . . . I have observed the misery of my people. . . . I have heard their cry. . . . Indeed, I know their sufferings, and I have come down to deliver them. . . . I will be with you." (Exod. 3:6-8, 12)

Long ago God spoke to our ancestors in many and various ways by the prophets, but in these last days he has spoken to us by a Son, whom he appointed heir of all things, through whom he also created the worlds. He is the reflection of God's glory and the exact imprint of God's very being, and he sustains all things by his powerful word. (Heb. 1:1-3)

How beautiful upon the mountains
are the feet of the messenger who announces peace,
who brings good news,
who announces salvation,
who says to Zion, "Your God reigns." (Isa. 52:7)

"Do not be afraid; for see—I am bringing you good news of great joy for all the people: to you is born this day in the city of David a Savior, who is the Messiah, the Lord. This will be a sign for you: you will find a child wrapped in bands of cloth and lying in a manger." (Luke 2:10-12)

Thus says the LORD: Are you the one to build me a house to live in? I have not lived in a house since the day I brought up the people of Israel from Egypt to this day, but I have been moving about in a tent and a tabernacle. . . . And I will appoint a place for my people Israel and will plant them, so that they may live in their own place, and be disturbed no more. . . . I will raise up your offspring after you, who shall come forth from your body, and I will establish his kingdom. He shall build a house for my name, and I will establish the throne of his kingdom forever. (2 Sam. 7:5-6, 10, 12-13)

The true light, which enlightens everyone, was coming into the world. . . .But to all who received him, who believed in his name, he gave power to become children of God. And the Word became flesh and lived among us, and we have seen his glory, the glory as of a father's only son, full of grace and truth. (John 1:9, 12, 14)

"For God so loved the world that he gave his only Son, so that everyone who believes in him may not perish but may have eternal life. "Indeed, God did not send the Son into the world to condemn the world, but in order that the world might be saved through him." (John 3:16-17)

For if while we were enemies, we were reconciled to God through the death of his Son, much more surely, having been reconciled, will we be saved by his life. But more than that, we even boast in God through our Lord Jesus Christ, through whom we have now received reconciliation. (Rom. 5:10-11)

> For a child has been born for us,
> a son given to us;
> authority rests upon his shoulders;
> and he is named
> Wonderful Counselor, Mighty God,
> Everlasting Father, Prince of Peace.
> His authority shall grow continually,
> and there shall be endless peace. (Isa. 9:6-7)

But when the goodness and loving kindness of God our Savior appeared, he saved us, not because of any works of righteousness that we had done, but according to his mercy, through the water of rebirth and renewal by the Holy Spirit. (Titus 3:4-5)

RESPONSIVE READING

Read responsively Psalm 98.

SHARING QUESTIONS AND INSIGHTS

Allow time for participants to ask questions or share thoughts that arose during their reading.

HYMN

Read or sing "Hark! the Herald Angels Sing." Look carefully at the words. Describe the subject of each stanza. What do you find surprising or puzzling about the hymn's message?

REFLECTION QUESTIONS

What help does the Christmas story give us in coming to know the adult Jesus and his ministry? in understanding the reason for his death? How do we see God's resurrection power at work in the Christmas story? What similarities do you see in the way God relates to human beings in Old Testament stories, in New Testament stories, and in our lives today?

Titus 3:4-7 uses several terms that we may let slip past us and fail to fully appreciate: God's loving kindness, Jesus Christ our Savior, God's mercy, the work of the Holy Spirit, justified by grace. Think about each of these terms in relation to the Christmas story as it unfolds God's love for humanity. How do we see God at work in the accounts of Jesus' birth?

What do we hope for? How do we imagine our future in God's household?

"Do not be afraid," the angel begins the announcement of Jesus' birth. Ask the participants to discuss what makes people afraid today. Ask the group to reflect silently and prayerfully, first, about the certain knowledge that God is with us; . . . then, about the Light of the world who comes to lighten our darkness, the Light that cannot be overcome; . . . and finally, about the Word of God made flesh, the Word that confronts and comforts, the Word of life.

What specific changes would you make in the way we celebrate Christmas in response to your understanding of who Jesus is and what he came to do?

TELLING THE STORY

Ask the group to put today's discussion in narrative form, so that it becomes a part of the whole story of the coming of Jesus Christ. Begin with these ideas: Jesus' coming as a baby, born to Mary, can be understood in the context of God's promise to come and be with the people throughout the scriptures. The angel, speaking to the shepherds, begins with the time-honored announcement of God's presence with us: "Do not be afraid." What is new in this story is that God becomes like us in the humanity of Jesus, willing even to die and rise again that we might have life in abundance. Use as part of the story the events and ideas alluded to in the hymn. End with this affirmation: "Christ has come; Christ is with us; Christ will come again."

CLOSING PRAYER

God, our Emmanuel, you have promised to live among us.

Embrace us with your love and give us peace; free us from all our fears. Give us this Christmas the joy of knowing you are near. Teach us to sing with the angels and rejoice in their song of peace and goodwill. Send us to those who long for your word of hope, and teach us to proclaim with the shepherds the amazing good news of Jesus' birth. Help us to know Jesus as our friend and brother and to see him as our Savior and the reflection of your glory. We give you thanks and praise for his coming. In the name of the Prince of Peace. Amen.

> Leader: The peace of Christ go with you.
> Group: **And also with you. Amen.**

Week 5

PREPARING

Prepare the room as in previous weeks, except use only one large lighted candle on the table. Have the words to the hymn and the psalm available for everyone. Find representations of Christ's reign from several cultural perspectives—art prints, photos of church windows, or Christmas cards—to tape to the board or easel.

OPENING PRAYER

Ask someone ahead of time to lead the opening prayer. Have index cards available for participants to list prayer concerns as they enter the room and give them to the prayer leader.

SCRIPTURE READING

Take turns reading aloud the following verses:

> Arise, shine; for your light has come,
> and the glory of the LORD has risen upon you.
> . . . .
> Nations shall come to your light,
> and kings to the brightness of your dawn. (Isa. 60:1, 3)

In the time of King Herod, after Jesus was born in Bethlehem of Judea, wise men from the East came to Jerusalem, asking, "Where is the child who has been born king of the Jews? For we observed his star at its rising, and have come to pay him homage." . . . When they saw that the star had stopped, they were overwhelmed with joy. On entering the house, they saw the child with Mary his mother; and they knelt down and paid him homage. Then, opening their treasure chests, they offered him gifts of gold, frankincense, and myrrh. (Matt. 2:1-2, 10-11)

Pilate asked him, "So you are a king?" Jesus answered, "You say that I am a king. For this I was born, and for this I came into the world, to testify to the truth. Everyone who belongs to the truth listens to my voice." Pilate asked him, "What is truth?" (John 18:37-38) Pilate also had an inscription written and put on the cross. It read, "Jesus of Nazareth, the King of the Jews." (John 19:19)

Jesus said to [Mary Magdalene], "Do not hold on to me, because I have not yet ascended to the Father. But go to my brothers and say to them, 'I am ascending to my Father and your Father, to my God and your God.'" (John 20:17)

> Give the king your justice, O God,
> and your righteousness to a king's son.

May he judge your people with righteousness,
and your poor with justice.

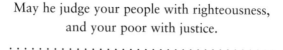

May he defend the cause of the poor of the people,
give deliverance to the needy,
and crush the oppressor. (Ps. 72:1-2, 4)

So he came and proclaimed peace to you who were far off and peace to those who were near; for through him both of us have access in one Spirit to the Father. So then you are no longer strangers and aliens, but . . . members of the household of God. (Eph. 2:17-19)

"Then the righteous will answer him, 'Lord, when was it that we saw you hungry and gave you food, or thirsty and gave you something to drink? And when was it that we saw you a stranger and welcomed you, or naked and gave you clothing? And when was it that we saw you sick or in prison and visited you?' And the king will answer them, 'Truly I tell you, just as you did it to one of the least of these who are members of my family, you did it to me.'" (Matt. 25:37-40)

[Jesus] said to him the third time, "Simon son of John, do you love me?" Peter felt hurt because he said to him the third time, "Do you love me?" And he said to him, "Lord, you know everything; you know that I love you." Jesus said to him, "Feed my sheep." (John 21:17)

For this reason I bow my knees before the Father, from whom every family in heaven and on earth takes its name. I pray that, according to the riches of his glory, he may grant that you may be strengthened in your inner being with power through his Spirit, and that Christ may dwell in your hearts through faith, as you are being rooted and grounded in love. (Eph. 3:14-17)

Above all, clothe yourselves with love, which binds everything together in perfect harmony. And let the peace of Christ rule in your hearts, to which indeed you were called in the one body. And be thankful. (Col. 3:14-15)

> "They will hunger no more, and thirst no more;
> the sun will not strike them, nor any scorching heat;
> for the Lamb at the center of the throne will be their shepherd,
> and he will guide them to springs of the water of life,
> and God will wipe away every tear from their eyes."
> (Rev. 7:16-17)

RESPONSIVE READING

Read responsively Psalm 148.

SHARING QUESTIONS AND INSIGHTS

Allow time for participants to ask questions or share thoughts that arose during their reading.

HYMN

Read or sing "Rejoice, the Lord Is King!" Look carefully at the words to the hymn. Describe the subject of each stanza. What do you find surprising or puzzling about the hymn's message?

REFLECTION QUESTIONS

Imagine the journey the magi undertook from their home to Bethlehem. Why do you think they set out? What did they bring with them? What difficulties faced them? How do we know they listened to God? What did they see in this child that made them kneel down and pay him homage?

What do we have a right to expect from a ruler or government official? How do you see the longing for a just ruler lived out in the earth's nations today? What prevents rulers from living up to their calling to be just, to "defend the cause of the poor," and to rule with equity? What characteristics of Jesus' rule can serve as examples for today's rulers?

Jesus' reign will redeem all creation and bring all of earth's people together. Share with one another ways meaningful to you that this biblical promise has been represented in art: paintings, poetry, music, stories, and movies. How does the celebration of Holy Communion show us the way to participate in Jesus' reign now? What other celebrations in the church year lift up this theme?

What other metaphors besides "king" can you think for Jesus' role as deliverer, ruler, and judge? Talk about these names for Jesus and what they mean for our lives: "Savior," "Servant of all," "Word made flesh," "Good Shepherd," "Lamb," and "Redeemer."

How do we as individuals acknowledge Jesus Christ as ruler in our own lives now? What are the benefits of letting Christ live in our hearts? What has to happen for the Holy Spirit to strengthen our "inner being" (Eph. 3:16)? Are there any aspects of our lives we have failed to give over to him? How do you identify yourself as a "new creation" in Christ?

Ask each person in the room to say what he or she anticipates from Jesus' coming.

TELLING THE STORY

Ask the group to put today's discussion in narrative form, so that it becomes a part of the whole story of the coming of Jesus Christ. Begin with these ideas: The prophets proclaimed that God would send a new king in David's royal line. The Gospels proclaimed that Jesus is this king sent from God. Jesus was called "king" by the magi and by Pilate. His kingship threatened certain people in power. Jesus invited the poor, the abandoned, and those deprived of power to be citizens of his reign. He became God's just ruler, coming as a servant, offering to be our shepherd, dying to free us from sin, and returning to God's right hand. Jesus urges his followers to participate in his reign of mercy and peace now, and Jesus will come again to call all people to his reign. Use as part of the story the events and ideas alluded to in the hymn. End with this affirmation: "Christ has come; Christ is with us; Christ will come again."

CLOSING PRAYER

Jesus our Shepherd, you have washed away our sins by your death and resurrection, and you have taken your seat above. We thank you for your gracious rule. Help us, like the Magi, to find you at the end of all our journeys; to recognize you as our merciful Lord, the ruler who guides us now and will gather us when the trumpet sounds in the home you have prepared for us. Give us courage to live in your reign now, welcoming the sick and the abandoned, defending the cause of the poor, proclaiming good news to the captives, teaching the ways of peace. Give us voices to sing your praise and rejoice with all the saints, for you have come to earth to lead all people to the brightness of your dawn.

Leader: The peace of Christ go with you.
Group: **And also with you. Amen.**

$\mathcal{D}on't\ miss...$

THESE OTHER ADVENT TITLES FROM UPPER ROOM BOOKS

While We Wait
Living the Questions of Advent
by Mary Lou Redding

If you are looking for a group Advent study with a difference, *While We Wait* offers new ways of connecting study participants with their own faith questions. Designed as a complete Advent study, this book offers readers:

- unique perspectives on the events of Christmas
- complete plans for small-group sessions
- a fifth session for the week of Epiphany
- daily scripture reading and reflection questions
- an introduction to the spiritual discipline of breath prayer

ISBN 0-8358-0982-X • Paperback • 136 pages

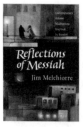

Reflections of Messiah
Contemporary Advent Meditations
Inspired by Handel
by Jim Melchiorre

If guilt creeps into your holiday cheer, you're not alone. Advent is the time to prepare for the arrival of the Messiah, yet most of us instead are swept away by the hyper-busyness of the holidays.

Melchiorre has found a personal antidote in Handel's *Messiah*. One holiday season, he turned to the familiar music and text to find solace from rampant consumerism. This simple exercise led him to find a way to intentionally observe Advent. His words will help you too.

IBSN 0-8358-9856-3 • Paperback • 128 pages

To order any of these titles, call 1-800-972-0433
or visit our Web site
www.upperroom.org/bookstore

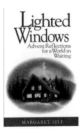

Lighted Windows
Advent Reflections for a World in Waiting
Margaret Silf

Have you ever read Hans Christian Andersen's *The Little Match-girl*? In the story, a poor little girl sees marvelous visions of the small luxuries life has denied her whenever she strikes a match.

Sometimes it takes looking at familiar seasons from a different perspective to be inspired again by the event. This book will help you look into your own "lighted windows" to rediscover "God with us" this Advent. Silf's observations are like the windows of an Advent calendar, leading you closer to the mystery that is born in Bethlehem.

ISBN 0-8358-9886-5 • Paperback • 160 pages

Child of the Light
Walking Through Advent and Christmas
by Beth A. Richardson

If the Christmas season has become more of a chaotic consumer ritual than a nurturing, spiritual one, you need this brilliant Advent survival guide! If you set aside just 10 minutes a day, *Child of the Light* will help you find your quiet center amid the stressful flurry of November/December busyness. As you read the brief readings inspired by the season's carols and hymns, your spirit will be lifted, and your thoughts will be redirected to the purpose of the season: preparing for Jesus' coming. Includes a small-group guide.

ISBN 0-8358-9816-4 • Paperback • 112 pages

The Night of the Child
Photographs from The Upper Room Museum
Nativity Collection
by Robert Benson

You won't want to miss this spiritual feast for the mind, heart, eye, and ear! Detailed photographs of the The Upper Room Museum's Nativity collection, along with scripture and Benson's thoughtful reflections, provide a fresh approach to the wonder of Incarnation. The visual images of Jesus' birth as seen by cultures all over the world remind us that God's love knows no boundaries. Order the book and the CD for a spiritual oasis during the Advent/Christmas season.

Book: ISBN 0-8358-0948X • Hardcover with Dust Jacket • 134 pages
CD with harp accompaniment, narrated by the author: ISBN 0-8358-0966-8

Notes

1. "How Can I Keep From Singing?" Robert Lowry, 1860.

2. Based on Zechariah's Song, Luke 1:77-79.

3. "Hail to the Lord's Anointed," No. 203, *The United Methodist Hymnal* (Nashville, Tenn.: United Methodist Publishing House, 1989).

4. "What Wondrous Love Is This," No. 292, *United Methodist Hymnal.*

Suggested Resources

The New Interpreter's Bible. 12 vols. Nashville, Tenn.: Abingdon Press, 2001.

Volume 6, Gene M. Tucker, The Book of Isaiah, 1–39; and Christopher R. Seitz, The Book of Isaiah, 40–66. (2001).

Volume 8, M. Eugene Boring, The Gospel of Matthew; and Pheme Perkins, The Gospel of Mark (1995).

Volume 9, R. Alan Culpepper, The Gospel of Luke; and Gail R. O'Day, The Gospel of John (1995).

Volume 12, Christopher C. Rowland, The Book of Revelation (1998).

Brueggemann, Walter, et al. *Texts for Preaching: A Lectionary Commentary Based on the NRSV, Years A, B, C.* 3 vols. Louisville, Ky.: Westminster John Knox Press, 1993, 1994, 1995.

Horsley, Richard A. *The Liberation of Christmas: The Infancy Narratives in Social Context.* New York: Crossroad Publishing, 1989.

Meeks, Blair Gilmer. *Season of Light and Hope: Prayers and Liturgies for Advent and Christmas*, Nashville, Tenn.: Abingdon Press, 2005.

Moltmann, Jürgen. *In the End, the Beginning: The Life of Hope.* Minneapolis, Minn.: Fortress Press, 2004.

Sloyan, Gerard S. *Preaching from the Lectionary: An Exegetical Commentary.* Minneapolis, Minn.: Augsburg Fortress, Publishers, 2004.

Stookey, Laurence Hull. *Calendar: Christ's Time for the Church*, Nashville, Tenn.: Abingdon Press, 1996.

About the Author

Blair Gilmer Meeks writes and lectures in the areas of worship and preaching. She is the author of *Season of Light and Hope: Prayer and Liturgies for Advent and Christmas*; *Season of Ash and Fire: Prayers and Liturgies for Lent and Easter*; and *Standing in the Circle of Grief: Prayers and Liturgies for Death and Dying* (all published by Abingdon Press).

From 1991–1998 Blair was editor of *Liturgy*, the quarterly journal of The Liturgical Conference and associate editor of *Homily Service*, a monthly ecumenical journal for preachers. She was also an acting coach in the chancel drama program at the Center for Arts and Religion, Wesley Theological Seminary and a teacher in adult education programs.

A graduate of Rhodes College with a B.A. in English literature, Blair has done graduate work at Duke University and St. John's University, Collegeville, Minnesota. She has taught classes in writing for worship at Drew University School of Theology and Montreat Conference Center and an M.Div. course in the Practice of Liturgy at Vanderbilt Divinity School. Blair is a United Methodist layperson, active in her local congregation.